"This book winsomely preaches the gospel without ever getting preachy. The authors use a series of contemporary life stories to illustrate what it means to follow Jesus authentically and creatively, and then weave together a description of faith that is simultaneously realistic, encouraging, hopeful, and compelling. This is the best and most refreshing discussion of what it means to be a Christian that I have read in years."

—Douglas Jacobsen, author of *Gracious Christianity: Living the Love We Profess*

"In *Faithful Witness in a Fractured World*, Johnson and Snarr lower the boom on an overheated discourse, making room for secular and religious people alike to think quietly about what faith lived in public means. They give us role models of decent, regular people taking their religious commitments seriously and doing tangible, real world good—not all at once, but bit by bit until kingdom come. This book is an inspiration, an antidote to being overwhelmed, and a reminder of the radical, transformational possibility that comes from doing small things with great love."

—Eileen Markey, author of *A Radical Faith: The Assassination of Sister Maura*

"What makes for an authentic Christian life? In this era of huge cultural, political, and social change, this book tells us how not to be a 'crappy Christian' and reminds us of the way to live into the Kingdom of God. Michael and Nicole introduce us to seven individuals whose vocations have been shaped by their understanding of Jesus' call to love our neighbors. This inspiring book shows how this enduring and radical life in Christ offers a way for personal and political transformation."

—Diane Randall, Executive Secretary, Friends Committee on National Legislation

"There are dozens of good books challenging us to care more about God's world, to be active, to make a difference. This one, though, is different—spectacularly so! In *Faithful Witness in a Fractured World*, Johnson and Snarr have given us a remarkably fresh and gracious guide to Christian social action by tracing the lives of a handful of what Shane Claiborne has called 'ordinary radicals.' In stories that are wonderfully told and prose that moves from elegant to sharp to cleverly witty, this book invites us all to learn how to be more civically-minded, how to care more for the common good, and how to emulate these friends of theirs who model this messy, glorious adventure of being God's agents of justice and peace. I am confident that there will be readers whose lives will be decisively altered for the better because of reading *Faithful Witness*. Quit complaining about 'crappy Christians'—find some friends, read this together, and live into a better story!"

—Byron Borger, Hearts & Minds Bookstore, Dallastown, Pennsylvania

"The dysfunction of our contemporary political scene is so overwhelming that it would be easy for Christians to throw up their hands in despair. But this timely book outlines a more faithful way forward. In the stories of a great cloud of witnesses—past and present, well-known and obscure—Johnson and Snarr find not only reasons for hope but also practical wisdom for the journey. This is an important read not just for individual believers but also for small groups and entire church communities."

—Heath W. Carter, author of *Union Made: Working People and the Rise of Social Christianity in Chicago*

"Thoughtful scholars teach us much about meanings in and through our Holy Scriptures, but with big hearts and sweet humor, Michael and Nicole give us a better gift. This book does not so much teach us as show us what Scripture looks like, in real time, in the flesh. The stories and testimonies are close to the ground and the biblical commentary close to the heart of Christ. I'm challenged, convicted, and encouraged. But most of all, I'm grateful for this project and the people of it."

—Noah Campbell, Associate Rector, St. George's Episcopal Church, Germantown, Tennessee, and Cofounder of Memphis Tilth

"One of the biggest obstacles to Christ is Christians, who often act very unlike the Christ we worship. Many folks love Jesus but don't want anything to do with Christianity because of the contradictions and hypocrisy they see in the church. This book forges the way towards a Christianity that acts like Jesus again, a movement that loves like Christ loves. Johnson and Snarr know that our current crisis in America is not just a political one, but it is also a spiritual and moral crisis. At the heart of that crisis is a church that has lost the art of spiritual formation. We've focused more on making believers than forming disciples, and when that happens our faith gets in a funk. Here's a book that can help us get out of the funk we're in and discover a faith that is worth believing in and dying for. This book is a call to love like Jesus loved, and not let the haters hold us back."

—Shane Claiborne, author, activist, founder of Red Letter Christians

Faithful Witness in a Fractured World

Faithful Witness in a Fractured World

Models for an Authentic Christian Life

NICOLE L. JOHNSON
& MICHAEL T. SNARR

CASCADE *Books* · Eugene, Oregon

FAITHFUL WITNESS IN A FRACTURED WORLD
Models for an Authentic Christian Life

Cascade Books
An Imprint of Wipf and Stock Publishers
199 W. 8th Ave., Suite 3
Eugene, OR 97401

www.wipfandstock.com

PAPERBACK ISBN: 978-1-5326-5314-8
HARDCOVER ISBN: 978-1-5326-5315-5
EBOOK ISBN: 978-1-5326-5316-2

Cataloguing-in-Publication data:

Names: Johnson, Nicole L., author. | Snarr, Michael T., author.

Title: Faithful witness in a fractured world : models for an authentic Christian life / Nicole L. Johnson and Michael T. Snarr.

Description: Eugene, OR : Cascade Books, 2019 | Includes bibliographical references.

Identifiers: ISBN 978-1-5326-5314-8 (paperback) | ISBN 978-1-5326-5315-5 (hardcover) | ISBN 978-1-5326-5316-2 (ebook)

Subjects: LCSH: Christianity and politics—United States.

Classification: BR115.P7 J65 2019 (print) | BR115.P7 J65 (ebook)

Manufactured in the U.S.A. AUGUST 26, 2019

Contents

Acknowledgments

So many people have been part of bringing this book into being. Below is a short list of all the totally non-crappy people in our lives who have been crucial to our work.

First and foremost, our thanks go to the seven models of Christian faith who have allowed us to share their stories with a wider public. We know that Paul, Julio, Tammy, Ron, Tessa, Emily, and Rick aren't *perfect*. But their unwavering commitments to neighbor love and their compassionate service in pursuit of a far greater good, which are grounded in the most sincere humility, make them perfect "everyday" models for the rest of us. Royalties from the book will go to support the organizations and projects to which our models are connected.

A lot of people helped in the logistical and technical aspects of interviewing our seven models of Christian faith. We are grateful to the staffs of the Westerville Public Library, the Wilmington Public Library, and the Wilmington College and University of Mount Union libraries. Thanks to Cara McEldowney at Mount Union for being our Skype-interview guru.

Particular individuals offered comments, critical advice, and encouragement at various points along the way: Glenn Griffin, Christy McNamara, Byron Borger, Melissa Snarr, Elise Snarr, Ruth Snarr, and Gethsemane Bray. The book is all the sharper for the careful reading and insightful comments of four amazing undergraduate research assistants: Keni Brown, Hillary Mitchell, William Martin, and Megan Canfield. Our editor at Wipf and

Stock, Charlie Collier, provided helpful feedback and support as we drafted chapters.

Writing this book has been a lot of fun, but it still required hard work. Our families deserve all the praise in the world for putting up with our periodically crappy moods at various stages. Niki thanks Glenn for his unwavering support and his patience with the 5:30 AM "time-to-get-up-and-write" alarm even on most weekends for the past two years. Georgia, Cecilia, and Noah deserve a heaping ton of gratitude for keeping their mother grounded in what really matters for a working mom of small children. Michael thanks his family for their patience while he was "working on the Jesus book" and with his seemingly unending conference calls.

The idea for this book was conceived in a First Year Seminar at the University of Mount Union entitled "Heroes of Faith-Based Social Justice." In the middle of considering the work and commitments and sacrifices of the big names—Martin Luther King Jr., Dietrich Bonhoeffer, Dorothy Day, William Wilberforce, Gandhi, Archbishop Óscar Romero, among others—students pause for a few weeks to find, study, and share with the rest of the class a "local" hero of religiously motivated social justice and change. That led to the idea of a book that would highlight regular folks humbly and faithfully living out their religious callings in less-than-conventional ways. Niki is grateful to her students over the years for introducing her to such inspiring models of faith—both Christian and otherwise. Michael's honors class on religion in public life served as a sounding board and gave greater shape to our ideas. Their feedback is greatly appreciated.

This book is dedicated to our students—past, present, and future—who strive to live authentic and compassionate lives of faith in difficult times.

Introduction

The Need for Models in the Present Moment—and Always

For I believe the crisis in the U.S. church has almost nothing to do with being liberal or conservative; it has everything to do with giving up on the faith and discipline of our Christian baptism and settling for a common, generic U.S. identity that is part patriotism, part consumerism, part violence, and part affluence.

~ Walter Brueggemann, *A Way Other than Our Own*

Then the King will say to those on his right, "Come, you who are blessed by my Father; take your inheritance, the kingdom prepared for you since the creation of the world. For I was hungry and you gave me something to eat, I was thirsty and you gave me something to drink, I was a stranger and you invited me in, I needed clothes and you clothed me, I was sick and you looked after me, I was in prison and you came to visit me."

Then the righteous will answer him, "Lord, when did we see you hungry and feed you, or thirsty and give you something to drink? When did we see you a stranger and invite you in, or needing clothes and clothe you? When did we see you sick or in prison and go to visit you?"

The King will reply, "Truly I tell you, whatever you did for one of the least of these brothers and sisters of mine, you did for me."

~ Matthew 25:34–40

A Short Intro to the Intro

The great Hindu hero and leader for justice Mahatma Gandhi once said, "Hey, I'd be a Christian too if it weren't for all the crappy Christians running around the place."

Okay, so Gandhi didn't say that. Not *really*. But he is alleged to have said something to that effect: "I like your Christ, but not your Christianity."[1] In our view, that's pretty much the same thing.

The tagline for this book developed out of a running joke between us. While we were working first on the book proposal and then on the manuscript, we would occasionally fall into fits of laughter, referring to it as "our little book on how not to be a sh*tty Christian." When our students caught wind of the joke, however, they insisted that we keep that as the book's title.

Thinking that they were just being edge-y, or maybe that it was funny to hear their professors confess to using bad words, we laughed off their insistence. And then we started getting the same response from older adults: "I'd definitely read a book with *that* title!" We compromised a little: it's a tagline, not the title or subtitle of the book, and we shifted to the word *crappy* so as not to offend *too* much. But alas, there it is, right on the cover: "How Not to Be a Crappy Christian."

If you're a little uncomfortable with the tagline, that's okay—we are too. But please know that it's not a gimmick or some crude ploy to get you to buy our book. (We're not keeping the profits anyway.) There's actually sincerity and seriousness behind the language. Despite our hesitation to use this verbiage in a book about something as sacredly important as religious faith, the

1. "Mahatma Gandhi," para. 1. The *Crimson* article reports that Gandhi said this to a Swarthmore College professor who traveled to meet Gandhi in 1927.

terminology does express our frustration with the current state of Christianity in America. If you're frustrated too, and if you can handle a little snark and the occasional reference to crappy Christians, we invite you to read on.

What This Book Is About

Like many American Christians, we are concerned with how Christian faith is playing out in the current political landscape and in American culture more broadly. The polarity and infighting among Christians over how (and even whether) to engage in the work of Christian mission and service seems more acute in this historical moment than it has been in prior decades. We suspect you know what we're talking about. Like us, prior to and following the 2016 presidential election, you've seen it on your Facebook thread and your Twitter feed, and if you're *really* lucky, you've experienced it right in your own family or friend group, at school or at work, and elsewhere: the ugly divisiveness that permeates everything from our news media to our dinner conversations. It is a divisiveness that makes assumptions about our politics based on our religious affiliations and vice versa, and which has the power to cut communication between family members and longtime friends. The divisiveness is exacerbated by social media as we create echo chambers of our own views by unfriending (and being unfriended by) those whose perspectives are opposed to ours.

As professors—one a politically engaged theologian and the other a theologically engaged political scientist—we admit that this situation leaves us concerned and scratching our heads. In our current American context, we wonder: what does it mean to live an authentic life of faith? How does one live an authentic Christianity in "Christian" America? Are Christians called to be in charge of the whole gig, legislating Christian morality and ensuring that the rest of our nation does not go too far down an immoral path? Or must Christians scrap the key tenets of biblical faith in order to engage politically or to bring a social or political position to the table? Given our current context, what is the future of Christianity in terms of its relevance and its capacity to create positive social change?

It seems to us that in the absence of real, widespread efforts among factions of Christians to bridge the divide, we need models to look toward for inspiration. That's what this book is *really* about. It's not actually about politics or theological perspectives per se. It's about people who, because of their Christian faith, have chosen the path of service and who pursue their work in somewhat less-than-conventional ways. They are individuals who are not famous for their work, and may never be beyond our telling their stories in a public way here through this book. They are in many ways "ordinary" people who have simply followed a path that most would find commendable, yet in the same breath would admit that their efforts are perhaps *too* challenging, or even "unsafe." And yet they are models that Christians from all corners of the political landscape can look to as models of authentic Christian faith and practice.

While Martin Luther King Jr., Dietrich Bonhoeffer, Dorothy Day, William Wilberforce, and other Christian activists for social justice and peace continue to inspire and move us to action, sometimes the lives and commitments of these "greats" can seem too radical (and their sacrifices too excessive) to be emulated. Certainly, we hope and pray for Christians to rise up in imitation of these extraordinary individuals who have changed the shape of world history for the better. But perhaps not all are called to that extraordinary path. Perhaps most of us are called to make significant changes in smaller corners of the world, or simply to make incremental changes for a particular community. The "heroes" we highlight here fall into these latter categories, but their contributions are no less noteworthy for being smaller in scale.

To be clear, we do not believe there is one right way to be a Christian in America. Yet certainly there are wrong ways to be Christian, a reality that we believe will become apparent as we move through this book. The point here is to highlight a handful of folks we have known or have come to know through our teaching, research, and civic engagement, and to showcase the example and witness of each as *one* sure way of being a Christian. We believe that regardless of political persuasion, the reader will agree that these are people whose commitments are inspiring and faithful—and in that agreement, we might find something to lessen the chasm between Christians in this historical moment.

Our goal, in the end, is not to offer something radically new, but rather to build upon foundations well established by other contemporary scholars and activists and the long tradition of Christian social thought before them. What we think *is* new is the *way* in which we attempt to offer some light in dark times, some clarity amid the confusion, some peace to counter the polarization.

Audience

While we have college students in mind as we write this book (since they're the ones we spend most of our time with), it's also for anyone who is interested in conversations at the intersection of religion, culture, politics, and social issues. As such, it's intended to be accessible even to those with little or no formal education in these fields. It's for people who are wrestling with (and frustrated by) the politicizing directions of Christianity and the developing factions within. It's also for those who may be looking for ways to best manifest Christian faith in our current American context and who are interested in different ways to think about the life of faith. It's about discovering one's sense of purpose and calling, it's about working for the common good, and it's about what Christians can be *for* rather than what they should be *against*.

We hope readers who lean to the political and social left will see that the gospel is not irrelevant. Jesus's message was very political, but not in a partisan sense of Republicans and Democrats and electoral processes in a two-party system. Jesus was political in the sense that he spoke about power and money and unjust social hierarchies; he was also concerned about the marginalized, the outcasts, and the "least of these," which meant that he clashed with the ruling authorities. To be called to work for justice is to be rooted in the teaching of Jesus. At the same time, we hope that those who lean to the political and social right might see the dangers of politicizing the gospel message and the subsequent blurring of the lines between what the gospel demands and what allegiance to America demands. In any case, and regardless of where you fall on the partisan political spectrum, if your view of the gospel automatically pits you against others and leads you to demonize your neighbor, we hope this book will lead you to reconsider that position.

All of that said, we don't believe that this is a book for Christians only; we contend that even a reader with no particular religious affiliation can be inspired by the stories told here. For a number of our models of faith-based social justice and change, their Christian faith is not blatantly on display; in fact, for most of them, you'd have to have an in-depth conversation to discover the faith that motivates and sustains their work, despite the fact that it's neither tangential to nor intentionally hidden from that work. Given the honest yet humble integrity of the models we showcase here, we believe that even the most ardent atheist might find their work commendable.

Our Approach: Assumptions and Foundations

This project is driven by a few general assumptions about what authentic Christianity is about—because if we're being honest, we do believe there are plenty of disingenuous forms of Christianity. The well-known advocates of Christian faith-based social justice have written about this reality: William Wilberforce in *Real Christianity* (1797), Martin Luther King Jr. in his "Letter from a Birmingham Jail" (1963), Dorothy Day in excerpts from her *Selected Writings* (edited by Ellsberg, 2005), Dietrich Bonhoeffer in *The Cost of Discipleship* (1937), to name a few. While we believe there are many ways to live one's Christian faith, we also believe, like those noted above, that any form of Christianity which loses sight of the Jesus Christ we find in the gospels is no true Christianity at all. Christianity is, we argue, most clearly Christ-centered (and thus most authentic) when it is prophetic, driven by humble conviction to serve others, and based on a radical ethic of love and compassion.

According to the Christian Scriptures, Jesus's public ministry begins when he stands up in the synagogue and reads from the prophet Isaiah: "The Spirit of the Lord is upon me, because he has anointed me to bring good news to the poor. He has sent me to proclaim release to the captives and recovery of sight to the blind, to let the oppressed go free, to proclaim the year of the Lord's favor" (Luke 4:18–19). In this moment, Jesus embraces a prophetic stance, rejecting any notion that faith is about riding out the unjust and crappy earthly existence one faces and trying to focus solely on the promise of a better afterlife. The path that Jesus offers is no "pie in the sky" religion concerned only about future grace and salvation; Jesus instead says he has come to work on that unjust and crappy existence *right now*, to give people a better present even as they await a heavenly afterlife. As Adam Ericksen argues, "For Jesus, Heaven is not essentially some place off in the distance where you go after you die. No, Heaven is a way of life to be lived right here, right now. We see this clearly in the prayer he taught his disciples: *Thy kingdom come, thy will be done on earth as it is in heaven*."[2] We'll see this prophetic understanding of Christian faith lived out by our models as the next chapters unfold.

An emphasis on the prophetic vision of authentic Christianity leads us to a second assumption about the essence of Christian faith: a commitment to service based on convictions of humility and selflessness. We believe that distortions of biblical teachings, such as the "prosperity gospel" and an overemphasis on individual morality as the sole path to salvation, distract from Jesus's example of outreach to the "least of these." Too many Christians lose sight of the centrality of service to the poor and disenfranchised as this concept is laid out in Matthew 25, where Jesus *explicitly* links salvation and discipleship to service to the stranger, the hungry, the sick, and the imprisoned. We believe that Jesus actually means what he says in the Sermon on the Plain regarding the poor, the hungry, and those who weep, and we take him at his word when

2. Ericksen, "Politics of Palm Sunday," para. 3.

he says that his followers will have to take up the cross and make sacrifices in service to those whom mainstream society deems worthless. The individuals we highlight in the following chapters live that commitment in inspiring ways as they serve a variety of poor, rejected, and vulnerable communities and groups.

Finally, we reject any form of Christianity that does not love. As noted above, if your religious convictions lead you to demonize others, there's a problem with your view of the gospel. Jesus's message is clear: "Love your enemies, do good to those who hate you, bless those who curse you, pray for those who abuse you" (Luke 6:27). We would argue that love is not passive, nor does it roll over in the face of injustice, acquiescing to the evil of oppression. We think about it like this: as parents, our love for our children requires that we correct our children's misbehavior and do all in our power to develop them into good, compassionate, kind people. Christian love requires that we do that for one another. Christian love also requires that we do the same for the systems and institutions that constitute our lives if we are to live that prophetic faith. But in all things, Christians are required to do that prophetic work with compassion, forgiveness, and mercy. As Miroslav Volf argues, "This, in the end, is what the Christian faith as a prophetic religion is all about—being an instrument of God for the sake of human flourishing."[3]

In the end, we see authentic Christianity as a *lived* faith marked by the virtues of truth, love, compassion, forgiveness, service, and sacrifice. To quote Ericksen again,

> The politics of Jesus seeks to influence our personal lives, but it also seeks to influence our political lives. Wherever personal or political systems use violence, power, and coercion to be triumphant and victorious, Jesus beckons us to follow him into a different kind of politics—into the Kingdom of God that lives and dies by love, service, and forgiveness.[4]

3. Volf, *Public Faith*, 5.

4. Ericksen, "Politics of Palm Sunday," para. 19.

Overview

Chapter 1 introduces the diverse group of people who have inspired us to write this book and whose commitments to and work for social action give life to the themes highlighted in the rest of the volume. They are diverse in age, race and ethnicity, political perspectives, and traditions within Christianity, and yet common themes and commitments connect their work. The stories of these models of Christian faith and social action—Rick, Tammy, Paul, Ron, Tessa, Emily, and Julio—are told in brief vignettes about who they are, the work they pursue, how they understand their calling to their work, and relevant theological, political, and social positioning.

Chapters 2 through 5 highlight four key themes or threads shared by our models of Christian faith and action. Chapter 2 explores the notion that authentic Christian faith is never passive but requires embodied, active work toward the common good. Although called to this work, our interviewees speak clearly to the ways in which their work is often tedious and unglamorous, and how small successes are the key to carrying on. We highlight the humility of these models of Christian faith and practice and the types of sacrifices (personal, social, financial, and other) they must make as part of their calling.

Chapter 3 considers the strength of our models' commitments to Christ and to Christian faith-based service and the ways in which that commitment has led them to an increasingly broad and inclusive ethic of love for different kinds of people. As their personal Christian faith deepens, their active concern moves further out beyond their own race and ethnicity, nationality, religion, and social class, and toward a more profound practice of inclusion. More specifically, this inclusive sense of love for and service to others is especially focused on marginalized populations and groups. It is noteworthy that, at some point in their lives, many of the individuals highlighted in this volume experienced exclusion by judgmental Christians and left the church, later to be drawn back by a more authentic Christian example of inclusive love.

Attention to the shared values of our models of faith continues in chapter 4, where we carefully treat the potentially controversial theme of allegiance and loyalty. In conversations with our models, we identify a particular orientation to Christ that eclipses loyalty to the nation-state. We note that they identify with different political parties and perspectives and yet, regardless of their identification as Republican, Democrat, or independent, they have come to a place of understanding kingdom citizenship as preemptive of national, civic, or other group identity and loyalty.

Finally, chapter 5 guides the reader through the models' collective understanding of their work as contributing to some degree to holistic redemption and restoration, working to connect this understanding to the great tradition of the "social gospel" and to other important theological traditions. Here we examine how our models of faith see their work as contributing to the larger narrative of the Christian story and the longer-term understanding of the biblical unfolding of history—or, put more simply, how they see their work as kingdom work, pursued "on earth as it is in heaven."

Conclusion

As Miroslav Volf argues in *A Public Faith: How Followers of Christ Should Serve the Common Good*, "In redeeming the world, God intervenes into the existing sinful world in order to transform it into a world of perfect love."[5] We believe that the call to all people who profess to follow the Christ of the gospel narratives is to participate in that redemption.

We don't think for a second that our slim volume is going to fix the fractures within American Christianity, let alone within our broken world. But we do invite the reader to be moved by a handful of unsung but inspiring people who, we believe, are getting it a little more right than a lot of others who profess to follow Jesus—ourselves included—each by modeling one way of

5. Volf, *Public Faith*, 46.

living out their faith in quiet, humble, compassionate Christian conviction. It is our prayer that, as you read through the following pages, you might find their witness as compelling as we do.

1

Meet Our Friends

Introduction

A decade ago, findings from a study by the Barna Group declared, "Christianity has an image problem."[1]

No kidding. And it seems even worse now.

We noted in the introduction that this book is about people, and that by engaging the stories of some really *good* people living out their understanding of Christian faith, we might begin to see what Christianity can be *for* rather than what it thinks it should be *against*. In our view, too much of current mainstream Christianity in America is focused on what Christians think they should oppose or even hate. But we know that the biblical descriptions of Jesus are very much about what, or more accurately *whom*, he was for: poor and marginalized folks, sick people, children, outsiders, and other voiceless, powerless individuals and groups in first-century Palestine. And he wasn't for them in some abstract theological way: he was *literally with them* in his ministry. Shane Claiborne echoes this when he says that the church desperately needs "lovers, people who are building deep, genuine relationships with fellow

1. Kinnaman and Lyons, *UnChristian*, 9.

strugglers along the way, and who actually know the faces of the people behind the issues they are concerned about."[2]

To this end, we invite the reader to meet some of our friends. In the next several pages, we travel to inner-city Pittsburgh where Christians are working to heal trauma victims, to the rural Midwest where a former drug addict is loving current addicts into a new life, and to war zones in the Middle East where a former horse trainer is defusing conflict one relationship at a time. We introduce you to a young woman who gave up a career in fashion in New York City to employ refugee women, and another working in Washington, DC, to bring together politicians from across party lines to address climate change. We've known some of these people for years, and others are relatively new to us, but each inspires us in significant ways with their humble and persistent service to broken or hurting people. These are the folks we look to when we feel inundated by the noise and bluster of crappy Christians. We share their stories hoping they'll inspire you, too.

Tammy Beery: Inviting the Stranger In

Do not neglect to show hospitality to strangers, for by doing that some have entertained angels without knowing it.

~ Hebrews 13:2

I was a stranger and you welcomed me.

~ Matthew 25:35

"I'm Tammy Beery and I am nobody special."

That's how one of our models of Christian faith and service, when asked, introduced herself.

Most of us have seen homelessness firsthand. From the safety of our locked cars, we see a homeless person on a street corner and try to avoid making eye contact, driving by in quickly forgotten

2. Claiborne, *Irresistible Revolution*, 295–96.

discomfort. Maybe we feel some sympathy—and a few of us might even respond in the form of some loose change or a spare granola bar—or we might just try to move on before we feel anything at all. Some Christians judge the homeless for the apparently poor personal decisions that landed them where they are. Even those who give are prone to only rolling their car windows down to the precautionary three inches—just enough space to pass out a couple of dollar bills and escape unscathed.

Tammy Beery took things further. A *lot* further.

Tammy's story starts out like so many other Christians. She was raised in a loosely Christian household and was taught to believe in God. Shortly after getting married, she moved overseas with her husband, who was in the Air Force, and lived there for a few years. In search of community, she found a church but soon discovered some gut-level concerns about what she was learning there, and that led her to begin reading and trying to understand the Bible for herself.

As Tammy explains it, she "surrendered" to God and became a Christian in 1990. For well over two decades, she studied the Bible, went to Sunday school and church, and "did what Christians do," but "without ever really connecting with people in need." In the summer of 2014, she began to see more homeless people, especially homeless women, along her town's main streets. They held signs that said things like "Will Work for Food" or "No Job, Need Money." One day, in the car with her husband, Craig, she noticed a couple with a baby who were homeless. Tammy was struck by the way the woman was hiding behind her sign in shame. Craig declared that the man needed to get a job to support his family. Tammy asked Craig, a hiring manager for an engineering firm, if *he* would hire this man, given his unwashed clothes and hair and no shoes. No, admitted Craig. He certainly wouldn't.

This conversation, along with the attitudes of people in her church, led Tammy to some new convictions about what it might mean to live out her Christian faith. As she read further into the Christian Scriptures, she began to see God's *active* concern for the widow, the orphan, and the foreigner. This, in Tammy's view, came to mean making room—literally—for the poorest in society. As Tammy puts it, God calls us "to be engaged and aware and empathetic with the suffering in our community." She began learning about homelessness and came to understand the connections between homelessness and addiction and domestic violence. Despite the view held by many in her circles that drug addicts were simply not their problem, Tammy kept returning to the notion that God continually calls people to take care of those in need. Tammy's compassion was multiplied as she heard the real-life stories of those who become addicts and eventually become homeless. As Tammy says, telling the girl who grows up with an addicted mother and comes of age mired in the world of drugs to "just get an education" to improve her situation isn't enough: "We just have to get off our high horses and care!"

A vision began to develop in Tammy's mind about what it would look like to live out this understanding of genuine, active concern for those facing homelessness due to drug addiction or other problems. She talked with a few local pastors and community leaders about her idea to provide shelter for homeless women. After multiple conversations with others in the community, a local judge who was working to develop alternatives to prison for drug offenders invited Tammy to present her ideas at a town hall meeting. Despite a near-panic attack at the thought of speaking publicly at the meeting, Tammy managed to share that vision with a group of pastors and other civic leaders. In particular, she noted the need for a "low-barrier" women's shelter that would not require background checks for admittance or turn away women who showed up high or drunk, as the vast majority of shelters do. By October 2014, just a few months after Tammy's initial convictions about serving the poorest in her community, Hope House, a low-barrier shelter for women, was up and running. Hope House provides overnight shelter for women and children who are the victims of domestic violence, drug abuse, and/or financial problems, and it operates from a Christ-centered perspective of care and concern for the "least" in society.

Tammy is relocating soon and has already begun to scope out spaces of need in her new community. She notes the difficulty of finding a church that is responding to God's clear call to serve the vulnerable and poor in society. The sad reality is that churches that function this way can be difficult to find. Tammy expresses frustration with the view that she is somehow special or unique, some kind of "super Christian" for the work that she does (recall how she introduced herself above). In her view, she is doing nothing more than responding to the call that God places on *all* people who claim to follow the Christian faith. This is a theme we'll come back to in the following chapters.

Ron Cordy: Leading Others to Recovery

Carry each other's burdens, and in this way you will fulfill the law of Christ.

~ Galatians 6:2

Do not judge, so that you may not be judged. For with the judgment you make you will be judged, and the measure you give will be the measure you get.

~ Matthew 7:1–2

Ron Cordy doesn't look like a "good" Christian. He doesn't always sound like one either. He's a big guy with a big voice and a rather gruff demeanor. He prefers to cut the sleeves off all his shirts. And he isn't shy about using four-letter words.

As a kid, Ron liked the Methodist church he attended. He acknowledges that his faith in God developed there and that he learned about love in that community, but he struggled to feel truly connected. One instance in particular stands out for Ron as indicative of the issues that made him feel that sense of disconnection. One morning at church when Ron was just a little boy, he overheard some adults making fun of the way another guy in church was dressed. They had welcomed this young man to church that morning and as soon as he was out of earshot, they criticized his appearance, laughing about his long hair, shorts, and sandals. This happened to be a good guy Ron looked up to and saw as someone who was really trying to live an authentic Christian life. At that moment, Ron glanced up at the painting of Jesus hanging behind the altar and saw the image of a long-haired man in a robe and sandals. The hypocrisy of men who looked nothing like Jesus (and wore polyester suits, no less—it was the 1970s, after all) poking fun at a person who actually bore some resemblance to him, coupled with the deeper hypocrisy of Christians judging other Christians for something as insignificant as their appearance, hit Ron pretty squarely in the gut. Negative experiences like this one confused and clouded other, more positive things he was picking up from his church. As Ron explains, this was just one example of the many times he saw Christians acting very un-Christlike, and he eventually left church altogether.

In high school, Ron made the acquaintance of Allen, his art teacher. Allen sometimes talked about his dream of opening a coffee shop and an arts- and music-focused space that would provide opportunities for ministry in service to the poor. At the time, Allen was in a successful Christian band that toured locally, and Ron would work occasionally as part of the band's road crew. Ron recalls thinking that Allen was wasting his time and talents by playing in a Christian band: "[I thought,] what an idiot, because I would be a rock star and I would make my own album covers . . . That's what I would do with my talents. . . . I sure wouldn't be [thinking about doing ministry with the poor and broken]."

Fast forward about a decade or so. Despite having a successful career, Ron began to live a lifestyle that eventually spiraled into alcohol and drug abuse. Things came to a critical juncture when he was arrested and convicted on felony charges for drug possession. Ron admits that, in retrospect, he is certain he would have met an early death if he had maintained the partying lifestyle, and he now looks back on that arrest as having saved his life. Rather than prison, his sentencing required mandatory recovery meetings for addiction. Flipping through a newspaper one afternoon, Ron saw a photo of Allen receiving a donation for his organization, Sugartree Ministries, and was astounded to learn that his former art teacher had realized his dream of opening a coffeehouse ministry. He visited Sugartree and discovered that they held a regular recovery meeting, so he began attending his mandated recovery meetings there. Eventually, as Ron began to overcome his own addictions, Sugartree asked him to oversee their recovery ministries, as well as the drop-in recovery house. For more than a decade now, Ron has facilitated the meetings, held twice each week, for people struggling with opioid, heroin, alcohol, and other addictions. He also sits on Sugartree's advisory board. Although the recovery meetings and pastoral support offered by Sugartree are Christian-based, people with any or no belief system are welcome.

Ron has stayed clean and sober all these years. He is still a songwriter and musician and directs his artistic talents toward the work of helping others stay clean and sober. He says that the one thing he is called to do is to love people. He becomes frustrated with Christian legalism, which is the overemphasis on rules rather than love and compassion. Did we mention that Ron sometimes uses some colorful language? This is one example that Ron uses to make his point: too many Christians judge others for things like using swear words, but then turn around and fail to love their neighbors, which is far more central to the message of Jesus. As Ron puts it, "We forget the root of it all, which is that we were loved, so therefore we can love. We were saved, so therefore we can help in the salvation of someone else, and not just in their soul but in their life." We'll revisit Ron's views of salvation and the church in the next chapters.

Tessa Reeves: Not "Business as Usual"

The foreigner residing among you must be treated as your native-born. Love them as yourself, for you were foreigners in Egypt.

~ Leviticus 19:34

All of our humanity is dependent upon recognizing the humanity in others.

~ Archbishop Desmond Tutu

At age twenty, Tessa landed an internship at *Elle* fashion magazine in New York City. That led directly to an internship at *Vogue*. She was on top of the world, having achieved these major steps toward her dream of a career in fashion design. Despite these accomplishments, she felt a growing sense of dissatisfaction with her work. This, coupled with a growing call to tangible love of the neighbor, would lead her down a very different—and far more fulfilling—path.

As an undergraduate student majoring in fashion merchandising, Tessa was lucky to land the internship at *Elle*. During that internship she had roommates, and the pace of work and life in the city kept her busy and excited about the work she was doing. When the work at *Elle* ended, her roommates left and she ended up living alone that summer for her next internship at *Vogue*. Living alone left her with more time for prayer, reading, and self-reflection. Two pivotal books for her during this time were Francis Chan's *Crazy Love* and John Piper's *Don't Waste Your Life*; both books push Christians to examine their lives more carefully and to make a full-on commitment to following Jesus.

Tessa was raised as a Christian and speaks with genuine gratitude for the solid theological foundation she received from her nondenominational church. But she also notes in retrospect that she often left church "feeling guilty about something." The messages she picked up at church focused primarily on what she was doing wrong and what rules she should be following. In college, prior to the internships in New York City, Tessa had found a church that emphasized the positive. As she puts it, "I left church feeling inspired to change and be more like Jesus" rather than feeling like religion was a "ticket out of hell." Tessa notes that in her home church, she had been taught to read the Bible directly and on her own—that she did not need an intermediary of any kind. In college, however, her mentors opened her world to devotionals and Bible commentaries. She began to realize that, while she could indeed approach the Bible herself, there were resources available to her that would expand her knowledge of Jesus and the Bible toward more depth and meaning. In her words, this really allowed her "to see Jesus' personality and his heart, specifically the mercy and humility" that jumped out at her when she read the biblical stories about him.

The books Tessa read in New York City that summer began to resound with her college experience of church. For the first time, she felt like she was exploring who Jesus *really* was. She delved into the New Testament to discover what the gospel narratives say about Jesus; her growing knowledge and understanding of Jesus, combined with what she was discovering to be a joyless workplace environment, had a dramatic effect on Tessa. One weekend that summer, she envisioned the end of her career: "I looked back and I tried to see what I had accomplished and it was all selfish ambition that I was chasing. My name was at the top of the masthead . . . but I hadn't really created any value for anyone else along the way." This, for Tessa, was a "slap in the face"; that week, she quit the internship, breaking any future relationship or opportunity with the giants of the fashion industry, and returned home.

With no plans or ideas about what would come next, Tessa worked to complete her degree the next year and began to do volunteer work to fill time. One of the volunteer opportunities was with an organization that brought her into contact with resettled refugees. The attraction she felt to working with refugee children and their families made it clear to her that she was in the right place, and she began to consider how she might build a career out of her growing passion for working with refugees. After graduation, she approached the organization for employment, telling them she would do anything, including office work, just to be involved. Instead, they invited her to partner with them in starting a business to create jobs for refugee women. In this work, Tessa would find a space where her love and talent for fashion met with her strengthening desire to serve the disadvantaged neighbor. This was the birth of Neighbors Apparel.

Neighbors Apparel is a fashion brand with the core goal of providing refugee women with sustainable employment and a living wage. As Tessa explains, refugee women often come from places where sewing and apparel-making are inherent in the culture;

sometimes these talents are further developed in refugee camps. Once they are resettled in the United States, there is no market for their goods. Neighbors Apparel provides additional training and the materials needed to create fashionable handbags and accessories and builds a living wage into the price of the item. The women work from home so that it is easier to care for children and other relatives. In Tessa's perspective, Neighbors Apparel is about helping refugee women to use their "God-given talents" in order to create goods for women who want to "vote for justice with their dollars." Tessa's business incorporated in 2014 and relaunched in spring 2018 with a new website and brand design.

Rick Polhamus: Loving the Enemy

Blessed are the peacemakers,
for they will be called children of God.

~ MATTHEW 5:9

We have never preached violence, except the violence of love, which left Christ nailed to a cross, the violence that we must each do to ourselves to overcome our selfishness and such cruel inequalities among us. The violence we preach is not the violence of the sword, the violence of hatred. It is the violence of love, of brotherhood, the violence that wills to beat weapons into sickles for work.

~ ÓSCAR A. ROMERO, *THE VIOLENCE OF LOVE*

Who in their right mind would give up a six-figure salary and some level of notoriety in order to walk into conflict zones and be a human shield? Our friend Rick would.

Rick is sixty-four years old and has worked for Christian Peacemaker Teams (CPT) for over two decades. He's inhaled more tear gas, ducked more shelling, and has had more guns pointed in his face than anyone we know. Yet when he talks about his work with CPT, these aren't the things that get the most attention. Instead, he likes to talk about people: sitting in the marketplace in Hebron and chatting with Jamal, a Palestinian architect with two doctorates who sells Bedouin goods because he isn't allowed to travel outside of Israel-Palestine; or Avi, an Israeli soldier who kicked and punched Rick on a hillside one day, was put on desk duty as a result, admitted to fantasizing about all the ways he wanted to kill Rick after that, and now meets Rick for pizza whenever he travels back to the Holy Land; or nine-year-old Adelia in Chiapas, Mexico, whose family took three thousand refugees into their small village of X'oyep when the military attempted to take over farmland and together were able to protect their land and lives through persistent and strategic nonviolent organizing.

It seems like fame and fortune were always on the horizon for Rick. In high school, he was a star athlete. He was named second team all-state in high school basketball and was drafted by the Kansas City Royals professional baseball team as a third baseman. Injury led to the end of his short time with the Royals, and he began training horses for a living. His technique was so sought after that it took him all over the world, and his methods appeared in a number of horse-training manuals. And yet . . .

Rick had decided early on that peace and justice work would somehow be part of his life and work. In their early years of marriage, Rick and his wife, Margie, maintained a continual thread throughout their conversations: "Kids don't deserve the world we're giving them, and someone needs to do more." Rick found himself having those conversations with the man in the mirror and eventually made a commitment to work for CPT, an organization that sends volunteer teams to places of conflict where they work to create space for dialogue and peacebuilding between clashing communities. Occasionally in this work, CPTers find themselves on the receiving end of a weapon or a fist, as Rick's stories attest, but the real work involves helping build relational bridges between sworn enemies.

In the same week that Rick accepted a contract with CPT, which provided a stipend of about two hundred dollars per month, he turned down an offer to train horses with a $100,000 salary. The reader might wonder at this point if Rick is nuts. Knowing him as we do, we'd probably say yeah, a little. You have to be just a little nuts, don't you, to be part of an organization that publicly announces its members are going to ride the buses in Jerusalem all day Friday following a series of Friday bombings targeting Israeli civilians on those same buses?

But then is it really nuts to follow your heart, your passion, your vision, your long-term sense of calling? This world tells us that what Rick did was irrational, because the world functions on the false belief that money and fame are the harbingers of happiness and the signs of success. But we'd argue that if we understand calling in the deepest sense of the word, then what Rick did was in fact *not* crazy, and what *would* have been crazy would have been to ignore the call that he felt to peacemaking. We explore this notion of calling more extensively in the next chapter.

Paul Abernathy: Transforming Neighborhoods

In all this I have given you an example that by such work we must support the weak, remembering the words of the Lord Jesus, for he himself said, "It is more blessed to give than to receive."

~ Acts 20:35

We have all known the long loneliness and we have learned that the only solution is love and that love comes with community.

~ Dorothy Day, *The Long Loneliness*

When Paul was called up from his Army Reserve unit in January 2003 as part of the first surge of the United States military invasion of Iraq, he couldn't have fully anticipated where the experience of war would lead him. His own encounter with war-related trauma, coupled with the trauma he saw in his fellow soldiers and in the faces of the Iraqi people as they navigated life in the middle of a war zone, led him to understand the implications of trauma in much broader terms. Eventually, he put that understanding to work in inner-city Pittsburgh.

Of course, forced to go three weeks in the desert without a shower, any of us might find ourselves reexamining the life choices that had led to such an unpleasant situation. But Paul had already been questioning some things in his life for some time, in particular the disconnect he felt between his reservist duties and his maturing Christian identity. Just before entering college, Paul had joined the military in order to pay for his education. But as he moved through that education at a small Jesuit Catholic university, Paul encountered ideas and influences that would lead him to some new insights into what it meant to follow his sense of Christian calling. He abandoned his plans for a lucrative career in accounting and switched to a major in international studies. He began to question his decision to join the military. He spent a year living in a service-learning community with other students, serving the poor in an inner-city neighborhood. And he spent a summer studying abroad, his interest in the Middle East and his Syrian lineage drawing him to the University of Aleppo in Syria.

It was in Syria that Paul, who had been raised Catholic, decided to explore the Orthodox Christian tradition. As he puts it, he was struck profoundly by the Orthodox beliefs and practices and "a sense of the mystical encounter with the living God" that he experienced there. He was attracted to what he views as the Orthodox tradition's desire not to dilute the teachings of Jesus even if they're hard to follow; specifically, Paul began to see a serious inconsistency in Western Christianity's propensity to profess to "love and follow Jesus" and its willingness to support and participate in the government's war-making and the killing of fellow human beings that war necessitates. Eventually, Paul would convert to Orthodox Christianity.

Not long after graduation, Paul found out that his Reserve unit had been attached to the Marine Expeditionary Force and would be part of the first wave of US troops invading Iraq in 2003. Even before that, Paul had considered filing as a conscientious objector and leaving the Army Reserve, but he knew that if he didn't follow through with his commitment, then someone else would have to go in his place. That didn't sit well with him, so he scrapped the idea. As an engineer, his work involved repairing bridges in the middle of intense gun battles between US and Iraqi forces. It was harrowing work, but even more troubling for Paul was his growing concern about Christian participation in war and his sense that he was a soldier in an unjust war. Upon return from Iraq, Paul joined a group called Iraq Veterans Against the War (IVAW) to voice his concerns.

In 2011, Paul began working with FOCUS North America, an Orthodox Christian organization that works to address poverty in more than fifty cities across the country. In his community development work as the director of FOCUS Pittsburgh, Paul began to see parallels between the trauma that war inflicts on both soldiers and citizens and the trauma experienced by those who live in poverty-stricken realities. In the first few years, says Paul, the emphasis was on meeting basic needs: providing food, furniture, clothing, travel assistance, and other necessities. He noticed that people would stop in for assistance of one kind or another but would begin to talk about the trauma they had experienced: seeing a friend or relative killed in the street by gun violence, being a victim of rape, or living with an addicted parent and having to wander the streets and fend for themselves.

In Paul's words, "I began to understand from those experiences that so much of our population was so deeply traumatized. In the army, they talked about post-traumatic stress disorder when we were overseas, which I had never heard of before, but I began to understand that there was so much more post-traumatic stress in my own community than I ever saw when I was in the army." Paul noted the concern for soldiers returning from war and their needs for healing from the violence of war, yet here he was in Pittsburgh, working with "children [who were] basically living their entire lives in a war." This realization led Paul to integrate "trauma-informed community development" into his work and to make it the main emphasis of FOCUS's efforts.

For Paul, working with FOCUS is very much a calling. But as he puts it, it is the calling of *every* Christian "to wrestle with the problems of this world." Christians are called to become more sacrificial in the lives they lead, which, he notes, is in direct competition with the idea of the "prosperity gospel" proclaimed by large swaths of American Christianity. At the core of the prosperity gospel is the notion that God blesses Christians with health and wealth—as if God rewards "good behavior" with money and material success. We will discuss these concepts more in depth in later chapters; for now we leave the reader to consider Paul's assertion that Christians must begin to "live our lives as pages of the gospel" wherein others might come to know God's unconditional love.

Emily Wirzba: Building Bridges

God saw everything that he had made, and indeed,
it was very good.

~ Genesis 1:31a

Genuine politics worthy of the name, and the only politics I am willing to devote myself to, is simply a matter of serving those around us: serving the community and serving those who will come after us. Its deepest roots are moral because it is a responsibility, expressed through action, to and for the whole.

~ Vaclav Havel

Few professions conjure a more negative image than that of lobbyist—someone who seeks to influence public policy by meeting with elected officials. A common image of a lobbyist is a wealthy man, representing a powerful corporation, banging his fist on a table in a back room and yelling, "If you want another campaign contribution and if you want to be re-elected, you will do what I say!" There is certainly some truth to this stereotype. Each year, corporations spend hundreds of millions of dollars to persuade politicians to serve the interests of their corporate shareholders.

So, if you met Emily, you might be shocked to learn that she is a lobbyist. The image described above couldn't be further from the truth for Emily, who works as a lobbyist for the Friends Committee on National Legislation (FCNL). FCNL is a different type of lobbying group. It is a nonprofit Quaker lobby in the public interest, which means it does not lobby in the financial interest of Quakers or those who work at FCNL, but rather for what FCNL perceives as best for society as a whole. As a Quaker organization, it also seeks to infuse its faith values into its policy positions. For example, FCNL works to reduce war and reduce environmental degradation—values that align with Quaker understandings of Christianity but that also serve the broader common good. It also works on behalf of groups that have been marginalized. Notably, FCNL is the only non-Native American lobby that works in the interest of Native Americans. There is no financial benefit for Quakers to lobby on behalf of Native Americans; the motive is simply a pursuit of justice for those who have been wronged in the past and continue to fight oppression. As the FCNL Legislative Representative for Sustainable Energy and the Environment, Emily focuses on federal laws related to climate change, sustainability, and the environment. This work enables Emily to put her values into action.

Emily was baptized in the Lutheran tradition but was raised in an ecumenical Christian environment that included time in a Kentucky Baptist church. Growing up in her church, she experienced genuine community and learned about the importance of caring for others. When her family moved to North Carolina, she attended the ecumenical chapel at Duke University. For most of her life, Emily knew she wanted to put her values into practice. In college, she majored in philosophy and political science and minored in poverty studies. She was concerned about a variety of social issues such as poverty and climate change, and she knew she wanted to make a difference in the world. Yet in her words, she didn't know "what my place in the world was." She was torn between wanting to make structural change and doing direct service work. To satisfy the latter, she interned at a homeless shelter. The work she did there was very rewarding, and she enjoyed working closely with the homeless population. She also had the opportunity to effect structural change through an internship with an environmental policy institute.

While she genuinely enjoyed working in both of these internships, she found "that when I was doing that direct service work, while I loved the relationship-building aspect of that work . . . my default position was 'well, why don't we change a law to fix that?'" That passion to fix broken and oppressive social structures led her to Washington, DC, to work with FCNL on issues of climate change and environmental concern. Each day, Emily works across the street from the US Capitol—the most important place in the United States for making structural change to protect the environment. The work of cultivating bipartisan political will to address climate change is difficult, says Emily, and involves working with legislators and their staffs to help them understand environmental concern as a spiritual and moral issue and to take more action. She is grateful for her work, which, in her words, forces her "to try to find the commonality and shared values with people in an era that is so partisan and hateful." If that's not reflective of kingdom work, we don't know what is.

Emily now attends a Methodist church in DC with a strong focus on direct action and advocacy—a church she describes as being known for "action in the world and the community." The church has a robust ministry to the homeless and other populations in need, which provides Emily with opportunities to pursue the direct action that she still feels called to by her Christian faith.

Julio Acosta: Loving the Least of These

Serve one another with whatever gift each of you has received. Whoever speaks must do so as one speaking the very words of God; whoever serves must do so with the strength that God supplies, so that God may be glorified in all things through Jesus Christ.

~ 1 Peter 4:10b–11a

A life not lived for others is not a life.

~ Mother Teresa

Julio is immersed every day in the work of social change, peace-building, and making the world better for every human. He exudes love for others, even for those involved directly in fomenting division and hardship for the communities he cares for most.

But as a Christian doing this work, he feels like a total anomaly.

Julio is an immigrant from Mexico who came to the United States when he was two years old and became a US citizen at the age of seventeen. It was the mid-1980s, and under the administration of President Reagan, immigrants who had come to the United States illegally were allowed to obtain citizenship. Julio grew up surrounded by the immigrant community, and his life has been shaped by the specific issues—and the often precarious existence—that immigrants face. Perhaps this life experience is part of the reason why Julio doesn't remember a time in his life when he didn't care deeply about others. This was just part of the fabric of who he was, even as a boy.

Julio's deep Christian faith has actually led him into interfaith work with an organization called Faith in Texas, which is a multiracial, multifaith movement that trains people in grassroots community organizing for racial and economic justice. Faith in Texas is part of the national Faith in Action network, formerly known as PICO (People Improving Communities through Organizing). Following an initial period of listening to the concerns of the local community, Faith in Texas determined that it would focus on justice issues such as education, immigration, predatory lending, and criminal justice reform. When Julio talks about his work, his passion simply spills over in explaining his plans—*big* plans—for organizing and helping people make a better world. He wants to teach people to be more strategic and effective through their advocacy, and he envisions organizing people locally to address local problems, at the state level for state problems, and so forth for national and global issues. (Did we mention Julio has big plans?)

All of Julio's commitments to working across racial, ethnic, and even religious boundaries to address these issues stem from his Christian faith. He likes to talk about the divine imprint in all human beings, citing the scientific research which explains our human genetic similarity to one another, despite superficial differences like skin color and other physical characteristics. For Julio, this is a calling. While he has wanted to alleviate the suffering of others for as long as he can remember—and thinks he would be serving others even if he wasn't a Christian—he describes his faith as filling him with the hope he needs to pursue this work. This faith-inspired hope enables him to keep working to make a difference in his hometown of Dallas, where change is slow, and in DC, where obstacles to change often seem insurmountable. His hope encourages him to meet with elected representatives who don't share his views. It keeps him from becoming angry and helps him look for places of agreement with those who disagree with him. In this work, he utilizes one of his best strategies: personalizing and humanizing the "least of these" on whose behalf he works. "The way to combat all this hate and anger . . . is with sharing stories" which can be used to bring us together. And since Julio believes that "no one is beyond redemption," he can sit down and converse even with his ideological opponents. Julio says it helps him to recall that Jesus, too, had to interact with people who disagreed with him, including the powerful Pharisees who tried to stand in the way of the tangible good he was bringing to individuals' lives.

So here's a guy working hard on behalf of the "least of these"—in other words, trying to follow Jesus in a pretty literal sense. Listening to Julio, one can't help being inspired by his thoughtfulness and passion. And yet as a Christian, he feels very alone. Despite having many friends and family members who are Christians, Julio does not find much support for his vision of a better world and his desire to tackle the major problems of our time. He knows some like-minded Christians—those with a strong faith and a conviction to help people on the margins—but the churches he has encountered seem more concerned with personal salvation: that is, getting themselves to heaven rather than loving others, especially those with the greatest need. "Where is the love?" Julio asks. "Jesus was a radical . . . He ate with tax collectors and prostitutes." For Julio, one can't love God without loving and caring for one's neighbor.

Perhaps the real irony for Julio is that he often sees secular groups caring more for those Jesus commanded his followers to love. And unfortunately, Julio often feels that his Christian faith is misunderstood or even unwelcome in those groups. It is interesting (and by "interesting" we mean horrible and confounding and pretty much the reason we wrote this book) that so much of Christianity has become so associated with hatred and injustice that non-Christians would scratch their heads, wondering why a Christian would be interested in positive social change for marginalized communities.

Conclusion

From our point of view, it's baffling that Julio—or any of the rest of the folks discussed in this chapter—would feel out of place in Christian communities given his commitment to try to live and serve as Jesus did. That's what Christians *do*—isn't it?

In one sense, there's nothing particularly "special" about anything that any of our models of Christian faith are doing. They're just living out what they view as a pretty straightforward response to what Christian faith demands. Unfortunately, however, too much of Christianity in the United States has been distorted to the extent that *just trying to actually follow Jesus* becomes something "radical" and worthy of study and analysis in a book. In other words, we look at these seven individuals with starry eyes, as if to say, "ooooh, they're so *self-sacrificial*, so *wonderful*, so *good*" when really what they're doing is simply what every Christian is supposed to be doing. It is, in a way, that simple, and this book is our attempt to address this problem.

We turn now to four chapters which constitute the majority of the book. Each chapter unpacks and explores one of four characteristics or perspectives common to these seven individuals: embodied, active faith; a Christlike love ethic; correctly ordered loyalties and allegiances; and a holistic understanding of redemption. These reflect at least some of the key biblical characteristics which, in our view, are indicative of authentic Christian witness.

2

Embodied Faith

You can find Calcutta anywhere in the world. You only need two eyes to see. Everywhere in the world there are people that are not loved, people that are not wanted nor desired, people that no one will help, people that are pushed away or forgotten. And this is the greatest poverty.

~ Mother Teresa

[Christians are called] to be in line with the witness of the early Christians, who even went and ministered to the lepers, putting their own lives at risk because for them, knowing who the Lord truly is, they were willing to lay their lives down by ministering to their brothers and sisters in need.

~ Paul Abernathy

Introduction

If you haven't noticed, the world we inhabit is kind of a mess. It has always been kind of a mess. Admittedly, it has been a bigger mess in certain places and at certain times than in others, but it has been a mess nonetheless. There is no lack of need in the world, and Christians are most definitely called to address those needs. That is in large part what it means to love one's neighbor: to help and serve others, to seek justice for the downtrodden, to live in a way that looks pretty different from the competitive, self-serving mode we see everywhere we turn. The Old Testament prophet Micah said it best:

> He has told you, O mortal, what is good;
> and what does the LORD require of you
> but to do justice, and to love kindness,
> and to walk humbly with your God? (Mic 6:8)

Those are *active* words: do, love, walk. From a biblical perspective, there's no room for sitting around, claiming to follow Jesus (another active word: "follow") but never getting off your behind to illustrate and embody what that looks like. As Jacobsen and Sawatsky put it in their book *Gracious Christianity: Living the Love We Profess*,

> The public purpose of the church is prophetic: to feed the hungry, clothe the naked, care for the weary, and ask questions about why so many people are poor and naked and weary. The church is called to analyze the world politically, socially, and economically; to question current structures; and to propose new strategies of justice and compassion. In a real sense, the church is called to be a community of the never-satisfied-until-all-are-satisfied, a community with hope that the power of God's love can remake both our own lives and the shared life of the entire planet.[1]

Among the many kinds of connective tissues linking the people you read about in the last chapter, one that we think is critically important is the notion that authentic faith is embodied, enacted, effective, lived out, worked out, tangible—pick a way of phrasing it, because any and all will do. What strikes us the most about each and every one of our models of Christian social justice

1. Jacobsen and Sawatsky, *Gracious Christianity*, 97.

is the concern for their faith to bear a certain kind of fruit: to make some kind of real change in this messy world, and to do so on behalf of those whom mainstream society has deemed as "less than" or otherwise undeserving of love, care, compassion, or protection.

Connected to this concern to bear fruit that leads to changed lives for others or to working for the common good is the notion of work as calling. To be "called" to something is different from "work" even if you really like the work. "Calling" is the sense that God has called you to a particular kind of work. (And let's be sure to note that by "work" we don't necessarily mean livelihood, or the thing we do that pays the bills; by "work" we mean to include activities like volunteering, hobbies and pastimes, and other things we enjoy doing.) The theologian Frederick Buechner referred to this sense of divine call as "vocation" and described it as the place "where your deep gladness and the world's deep hunger meet."[2] And for the record, neither Buechner nor the models highlighted in this book would contend that to be "called" means never feeling frustrated or exhausted by the work; it simply means that, for the most part, you not only employ your talents joyfully while doing the work, but you also recognize your work as contributing to some greater good rather than just receiving self-serving ends from it. In this chapter, we start with an exploration of Christian calling or vocation in order to ground and then showcase these models' examples of embodied, active, authentic faith.

Calling: Work as Vocation

An Understanding of Calling

To what—and to whom, we might ask—are Christians called? Let's take a moment first to consider the idea of "calling" or "vocation"—or what we might just call *purpose*—in a broader sense.

In their anthology *Leading Lives That Matter: What We Should Do and Who We Should Be*, Mark Schwehn and Dorothy

2. Buechner, *Wishful Thinking*, 95, quoted in Schwehn and Bass, *Leading Lives That Matter*, 112.

Bass gather together a large collection of readings spanning centuries of wisdom about the human quest for meaning through our work as well as "the other vitally important parts of lives that matter—love and friendship, family and sexuality, leisure and play, study and worship."[3] As they note, "Many young people experience a . . . yearning for work that is meaningful and significant. So do millions of somewhat older people who feel that their current employment is not satisfying in this regard."[4] But it is not just meaning that people yearn for: "Many people today desire . . . to lead lives that are meaningful but also significant, lives that manifest both personal integrity and social responsibility."[5] And so work—along with the other activities we engage in that constitute our lives—is ideally about more than paying the bills, growing rich or powerful, or making our way to the top. A true sense of vocation or calling may possibly include some of those things, but it needs to and should be connected much more fully to our sense of identity and who we are. This is what StoryCorps founder David Isay is getting at in his book *Callings: The Purpose and Passion of Work* when he says that "finding what you're meant to do with your life has a lot to do with careful listening—to that quiet voice inside that speaks to *who you really are*."[6] Schwehn and Bass also emphasize the notion of identity: "We sense that what we do to earn a living somehow emerges from *who we really are*, and we also sense that what we do to earn a living will somehow shape who we will be. A person's thinking about what to do to earn a living, in other words, is entangled with her identity and how she understands it. A person's choice of livelihood is framed by a sense of who he is and what he hopes to become as a particular human being."[7]

One thing that rings true across the board for our models of Christian faith highlighted in this book is the perception of calling

3. Schwehn and Bass, *Leading Lives That Matter*, 3.
4. Schwehn and Bass, *Leading Lives That Matter*, 1.
5. Schwehn and Bass, *Leading Lives That Matter*, 2.
6. Isay, *Callings*, 4.
7. Schwehn and Bass, *Leading Lives That Matter*, 2. Emphasis added.

or purpose that is based very much upon their sense of identity and knowing who they are at their very core—people who were first loved by God and are called in turn to love others. When people know who they are and live their lives out of that knowledge and identity, they are able to live with integrity and wholeness, serving others with compassion and a view to the common good. (And a nice side effect of living with integrity and wholeness is that, when you near the end of your life, you rarely look back on that life with any big regrets about how you lived it.) In our experience, conversations among Christians about calling, vocation, and purpose are too few and far between. Like the broader culture, we focus on the amount of money we'll make, the notoriety or power or influence we'll achieve, or some other kind of personal benefit. We too seldom consider whether the work we want to do will benefit or harm other people, how our work may be complicit in negative social, environmental, or economic outcomes for others, or how the values of the company or institution or field we're working in are actually misaligned with—or even in direct opposition to—our Christian values.

The friends featured in this book have a clear sense that their identity is bound up with the narrative of a poor homeless guy from first-century Palestine and the community that he loved and founded and brings to fruition in the fullness of time. That's not to say, of course, that our models have "arrived" at being the Best Christians Ever. But their identities as people who follow Christ are such that they are seeking intentionally to understand what that means in a truer sense. Those of us who call ourselves "Christian" absolutely must work to do the same thing. The work of discerning Christian identity is a pretty big deal, and American Christians spend far too little time talking about Christian identity—by which we mean authentic, Jesus-first Christian identity—and what that means for our individual and collective sense of calling and purpose. In the wake of our failure to allow Christ to shape our identity uniquely, we tend to allow other identities and ideas to shape our faith, which almost always waters down or subverts the gospel message. We think Shane Claiborne hits the proverbial nail on the head: "Beyond knowing that God has a purpose for our lives, most of us . . . spend little energy seeking our vocation, especially in light of how the needs and sufferings of our neighbors might inform how we use our gifts for divine purposes."[8]

This all brings us back to the question at the start of this section: To what—to whom—are Christians called?

Theologians and thinkers, pastors and priests, and lots of other Christian writers, teachers, and activists have been asking and answering this question in various ways for two millennia. The best answers, in our view, are those that align with the person of Jesus we meet in the gospel narratives. We don't know of any more genuine or more straightforward and simple ways to discern what it is that Christians are called to than to look to the work and activity of Jesus as outlined in the gospels. And in really simple terms, Jesus *did* two major things: 1) he gave hope to an oppressed people (the Jews of Palestine) suffering under the oppressive Roman Empire, and 2) he manifested God's love, compassion, and concern for all the folks who, in his era, weren't considered worthy of the time or energy of the more privileged people in Jewish society: women, sick people, children, beggars, non-Jews, and the disabled. Far too many Christians either forget or ignore this central activity of the person they claim to follow.

It's one really significant thing that he cared tangibly for the outcasts of society, talking with them, healing them, giving them hope. But the guy even sat down for meals with people like tax collectors: those Jews who were considered to be full-on traitors to the cause of a free Palestine because they colluded with the oppressor Roman government to collect taxes from the Jews. Imagine the hatred you'd have for a member of your community whose job it was to take money from you and turn that money over to the people who are preventing your freedom. Imagine a Messiah who works lovingly and compassionately to help those same tax collectors see that they are not called to any kind of work that oppresses others. It is a pretty deep and profound love

8. Claiborne, *Irresistible Revolution*, 138.

for all people that leads Jesus to hang out with those tools of your oppression in order to help them see the light.

This should signal to Christians in a big way that we are called to something really, *really* different from what mainstream culture looks like—whether that's first-century Palestine or twenty-first-century America. Christians are called to discern a unique identity and purpose rather than just follow along with what the rest of the culture is doing. In living into that identity and purpose, which is about embodying Jesus's love for others in compassionate service, we will likely find ourselves existing in opposition to the broader culture. We need look no further than the founder of our tradition to know and understand that. If we don't, we pass over the gospel narratives and fail to embody the teachings of Jesus. It's pretty hard to embody something you don't know about. In other words, it's hard to be a Christian if you haven't taken the time to understand what and whom the founder of the faith cares about as expressed in the biblical account of that founder. Sometimes, the words and actions of people who call themselves "Christians" are so far from who Christ is that it's no wonder non-Christians see little more than hypocrisy when they look at the church, and therefore want nothing to do with it. People tend to be able to see right through a lack of integrity, and certainly there's little integrity embodied in the person who professes to follow Christ—a man whose entire ministry was based on caring for the "least of these" with utmost humility and compassion—but then engages in hateful words or actions against others. As Will Willimon and Stanley Hauerwas put it, the true church

> calls people to conversion, but it depicts that conversion as a long process of being baptismally engrafted into a new people, an alternative polis, a countercultural social structure called church. It seeks to influence the world by being the church, that is, by being something the world is not and can never be, lacking the gift of faith and vision, which is ours in Christ. The confessing church seeks the visible church, a place, clearly visible to the world, in which people are faithful to their promises, love their enemies, tell the truth, honor the poor, suffer

for righteousness, and thereby testify to the amazing community-creating power of God.[9]

Sacrifice as Central to Authentic Christian Calling

So if we've convinced you that Christians are uniquely called to embody Christian love and service and related ideals in ways that look different from the rest of our culture, it's time for a reminder that choosing to follow Christ comes with a cost—sometimes, a pretty major cost. Does discovering or discerning one's calling as a Christian mean that we never face tough times? Of course not. In every long-term endeavor, it would be totally unrealistic to expect that we'll never have a day that doesn't confound us or experience a part of the work we don't like. Think of it like a really great friendship or dating or marital relationship: even the best of those relationships involves moments and even seasons that are frustrating or unpleasant. In those really great relationships, sometimes it's the working-through of those moments and seasons that makes the relationship even stronger on the other side. One could say the same for our sense of vocational calling: sometimes it's in the difficult, lonely, or even downright unpleasant aspects of the work that we recognize the good about that calling overall.

Let's delve a little further into this "underside" of Christian vocation and calling, shall we? There's no sense pretending that following Jesus is all sunshine and roses. Our models of authentic Christianity are clear in their agreement that Christian faith is not about prosperity and "blessedness," at least not as mainstream American culture understands those terms. Jesus doesn't reward "good behavior" with wealth and social status. That's the way the world works, not the Christian community, and our models' lives offer a serious critique of any allegedly "Christian" theology that says the sign of true faith is money, good health, influence, power, or even generalized happiness. Our friend Paul explains that, when one has an authentic faith experience, a "mystical encounter" with the living God, one comes to see with clearer eyes what it means to

9. Hauerwas and Willimon, *Resident Aliens*, 46.

be a Christian, and there is no room for believing that being called by God equates to an easy, self-satisfying path:

> That mystical encounter with the living God really informs what we do [at FOCUS Pittburgh]. . . . People sometimes think that, as Christians, we can do good work and build social services, we can help people, we can feed people, and we can work against injustice like a lot of people do, but there's something different about it if it's really inspired by an encounter with the living God. . . . [A true Christian] is one in whose life you can see the living God [and] what we really need is more theologians in this sense. Many Christians can study the Scriptures, get advanced degrees in the Scriptures or divinity, but if we do this without really knowing God, then we do so serving our own interests. But when it's rooted in a mystical encounter with God, we ourselves become more sacrificial in the lives that we lead. In this day and age when we have this competing prosperity gospel, where [people believe] the Lord wants us to have good businesses and wealth and all this, we are really missing the words of Jesus: "Whosoever does not deny himself, take up his cross, and follow me is not worthy of me" [Matt 10:38]. [Christians are called] to be in line with the witness of the early Christians, who even went and ministered to the lepers, putting their own lives at risk because for them, knowing who the Lord truly is, they were willing to lay their lives down by ministering to their brothers and sisters in need. And of course this expression of God's unconditional love made their lives as pages of the gospel, and I think this is really what a lot of us here hope: for our lives to become as pages of the gospel, where people can know by our lives that they're loved by God.

As Paul's reflections remind us, Jesus himself made it very clear that following him involves sacrifice, "bearing the cross," and even facing the hatred of those who don't share faith in him. Leafing through the pages of Christian history, we learn from those Christian movers and shakers who made the most significant lasting social change just how much Christians are sometimes called to sacrifice when they feel the call of the divine and seek to follow Jesus genuinely. And although this book is about "regular" folks who can serve as models of Christian faith and witness in a time of deep political and social division, a quick catalogue of the kinds of sacrifices some of those more well-known social justice heroes have made helps drive home the point that there is indeed a cost to closely following Jesus.

Dietrich Bonhoeffer

As the German Christian Church got sucked into Nazi ideology under Hitler's rule in the 1930s, a small handful of German pastors and theologians said, "Hold up, everyone. Our allegiance is to Jesus Christ—not the Third Reich government." That sentiment became the basis of the Barmen Declaration, a document that laid out the biblical foundations for loyalty to Christ *alone*, over and above any earthly political or social order. In turn, the Barmen Declaration initiated what was called the Confessing Church—as in confessing Jesus as Lord above all other lords. Bonhoeffer stayed true to the Confessing movement even as the threats to his well-being and that of his fellow Confessing Church pastors and theologians increased. And, well, you probably know what happened not only to the Jews but to anyone who stood against Hitler: Bonhoeffer was arrested in April 1943, imprisoned for two years, and in April 1945 was hanged in a concentration camp for treason.

Archbishop Óscar Romero

Father Óscar Romero was chosen as archbishop of El Salvador in 1977 precisely because he was thought to be a nerdy bookworm who wouldn't interfere in the violence being waged by the Salvadoran government against the poor—a conflict ignored and even enabled by the upper levels of the Salvadoran Catholic Church at that time. But when his fellow priest and friend, Fr. Rutilio Grande, was murdered in cold blood by the paramilitary for standing on the side of the poor, Romero was converted to the side of the oppressed and began to speak against the brutality of the government. He chose to live among and serve the poorest people of El Salvador—those who were simply trying to eke out an existence and follow their Christian faith. Once again, you're probably familiar with what happens when people speak up against power, especially in a militarized, authoritarian regime: he was mown down by a paramilitary gunman in the middle of leading worship in a hospital chapel. It should be of no small discomfort to the reader to know that Romero's killer was trained in those assassin's techniques at the School of the Americas in Fort Benning, Georgia.

William Wilberforce

William Wilberforce was a member of British Parliament for decades spanning the late 1700s and early 1800s. Wilberforce's childhood pastor, John Newton, had been a slave trader before his conversion and later wrote the well-known Christian hymn "Amazing Grace." Over the years, Wilberforce remained close to Newton, who mentored and encouraged Wilberforce as he moved into political leadership. As an adult, Wilberforce developed an obsession with abolishing the slave trade, and with the help of a like-minded, abolitionist Christian community of friends and associates, he is considered to be responsible for finally getting legislation passed in England that permanently ended the slave trade. That process took decades, however, and Wilberforce sacrificed his physical (and at times mental) health working in response to what he understood as an unequivocal call by God to end the sin-ridden practice of enslaving fellow human beings. Despite incredible frustration throughout the years and the physical toll that stress took on his bodily health, Wilberforce persevered in his Christian calling to end slavery.

Dorothy Day

As the founder of the Catholic Worker, a movement that established both a newspaper geared to the cause of the poor and to workers' rights and houses of hospitality for homeless and other destitute individuals, Dorothy Day devoted decades of her life to service. She lived incredibly simply alongside those she served, foregoing the conventional, "normal" path of a husband and a home of her own. She instead raised her daughter, Tamar, in the confines of a poor, overcrowded New York City neighborhood—a tension that is explored to some degree in the film *Entertaining Angels: The Dorothy Day Story*. In later years, she was arrested several times for nonviolent civil disobedience against nuclear armament and other issues that she saw as an affront to the needs of the poor. Day writes in her aptly titled autobiography, *The Long Loneliness*, about being called to this life of service and voluntary poverty, but acknowledges that such a life is marked by times of serious difficulty, disappointment, and even self-doubt.

So *this* is the cost of discipleship. Note that we said the *cost*, not the *reward*, of discipleship. Again, the God of Jesus Christ is not a God who rewards good behavior. We can't state this strongly enough. Dietrich Bonhoeffer wrote about this in his classic work by the same title, *The Cost of Discipleship*, where he differentiates between "cheap" and "costly" grace: "Cheap grace is the preaching of forgiveness without requiring repentance, baptism without church discipline, Communion without confession, absolution without personal confession. Cheap grace is grace without discipleship, grace without the cross, grace without Jesus Christ, living and incarnate."[10] Costly grace, in contrast, is about "the call of Jesus Christ at which the disciple leaves his nets and follows him. . . . Such grace is *costly* because it calls us to follow, and it is *grace* because it calls us to follow *Jesus Christ*. It is costly because it

10. Bonhoeffer, *Cost of Discipleship*, 44–45.

costs a man his life, and it is grace because it gives a man the only true life."[11]

Lest the reader begin to think, "Well, if the cost of living authentic Christian faith is *that* high, then forget it," we offer a reminder from the Gospel of Matthew: "Take my yoke upon you, and learn from me; for I am gentle and humble in heart, and you will find rest for your souls. For my yoke is easy, and my burden is light" (Matt 11:29–30). People who have lived long enough know that the secret to contentment is knowing that "the good life" isn't about worldly success and an easy path; it's about having worked hard to achieve something or reach their goals, but doing so with integrity. It's about being selfless, living for others, embodying the good, and being a part of something that is much bigger than our individual lives.

Our models' stories and perspectives illustrate the connection of sacrifice to embodied faith over and over again. For Tessa, actively following her sense of calling meant giving up a dream job in fashion. Recall that she was in the midst of living out her dream in New York City, having started a second internship with a major fashion magazine, when she had a flash-forward of sorts about her life and envisioned feeling empty and unfulfilled if she continued down the career path she was on. And there's Rick, who, in the same week in which he committed to the work of peacemaking with Christian Peacemaker Teams at a stipend of two hundred dollars per month, gave up a six-figure salary training

11. Bonhoeffer, *Cost of Discipleship*, 45. It is our view that far, far too much of American Christianity has lost sight of this call to costly discipleship. Instead, we preach prosperity and blessedness, and our churches look like monochrome, socially and economically stratified country clubs and civic groups. In turn, we have become people who criticize those of a different race, ethnicity, sexual orientation, economic class, political persuasion, ethical perspective, or even geographical location without a clue about who they are, what they really believe, or why they believe it. We leave no room for nuance, and our ignorance of one another creates space to be filled by our prejudices and assumptions. That's not the body of Christ in any real sense of the phrase. One of the easiest and most effective things contemporary American Christians can do is sacrifice a little time and energy to get to know Christians with whom they don't think they see eye to eye.

and racing horses. Emily, in her work as a lobbyist for the protection of God's creation, faces the frustration and constant threat (sometimes turned reality) that any success she and her associates might achieve on behalf of the environment will be rolled back with changing political leadership. At various times and to varying degrees, our models of embodied Christian faith have sacrificed time, money, comfort, relationships, reputation, and opportunity. Their work can be unglamorous and even boring at times, but a few success stories, along with that strong feeling of being called to the work, affirm their work as truly meaningful and fulfilling.

So what's the point here? Everybody makes sacrifices in their lives, right? But the sacrifices these folks have made and continue to make are borne directly out of their call to embody their Christian faith in unique, though not necessarily extraordinary, ways. King, Day, Romero, Bonhoeffer—they're all incredibly inspiring, and they are and will remain people to whom the Christian community should look as authentic models of Christian faith, service, and social justice. But we recognize how daunting it can feel to try to emulate some of these "greats" whose contexts were so different from that of most American Christians. Not all Christians are called to be martyrs, nor to live in total voluntary poverty—the ministry of Jesus himself was supported by women with some degree of wealth who were committed to his cause. That's not to let Christians off the hook, but rather to encourage you to consider carefully what sacrifices you are perhaps being asked to make in order to more closely follow a true Christian path.

We want to make one other thing clear here: this book is not about guilt or judgment. Good heavens, we have enough of that in American Christianity, and the last thing we want is to sound like we're telling people that they're not *doing* Christianity rightly or that they should feel guilt in comparison to the people we're highlighting here. We wish we'd kept track of the number of times we've said to one another, somewhere between half-joking and totally serious, "Wow, we really suck as Christians, don't we?" in the process of writing this book. There have been times when the two of us have felt really convicted about our own lifestyles and relative wealth and privilege, and we too have experienced many moments of considering whether we're sacrificing enough or sufficiently embodying the faith we profess. We recognize in our own lives all the ways we fail to be "as pages of the gospel," to use Paul's words above, and we are painfully aware of how much better we could be doing in terms of embodying our faith. But while we know we need to keep working on it, we also keep coming back to the notion that it takes all kinds of people and callings to create authentic Christian community, and we really like Shane Claiborne's words related to this: "The incredible thing is that the stories of ordinary radicals are all over the place, stories of everyday people doing small things with great love, with their lives, gifts, and careers. . . . The examples are as numerous as the number of vocations. But the calling is the same: to love God and our neighbors with our whole lives, careers, and gifts."[12]

Maybe we're not all called to be Bonhoeffers, or Days, or Romeros—but maybe if the majority of people who appropriate the label "Christian" could strive to be Tammys or Julios or Pauls, the witness of the church wouldn't confound our non-Christian friends and neighbors so much. We are called—clearly—to love the unlovable. That's just *biblical*, for crying out loud. What that love looks like is debatable, of course, and this may be what Christians on the political right and left fight about more than anything. But what is nonnegotiable—and we don't think that's too strong a word—is that if you say you're a Christian, you need to discern and pursue Christian calling, making real sacrifices on behalf of "the least of these," with whom Jesus identified more than any other group.

Embodied Faith and Discipleship in Community

During our conversation with her, Tammy told us a story that continues to resonate with us as we think about the Christian community and its importance for the other topics we've covered in this

12. Claiborne, *Irresistible Revolution*, 137–38.

chapter so far. Tammy recalls an instance when a woman at a nail salon asked her what she did for a living. Tammy explained her work with Hope House, the women's shelter she started in 2014 for victims of domestic violence, drug addiction, and financial problems. The woman mused aloud whether "those people" wouldn't "just be better off dead." In response, Tammy described a heart-wrenching story of a boy growing up with drug-dependent parents, outlining his life from kindergarten through high school, to explain to the woman how it is that an innocent child might grow up to find a sense of comfort, belonging, and community through drug use when all other communities (school, peer friendships, family, etc.) have failed him and ostracized him during his younger years. For Tammy, "if the church can't be a community for that kid, then lock the doors and go home."

Can we get an "Amen"?

Our last task in this chapter is to spend a little time talking about the importance of Christian community for building the capacity to embody and live out our Christian faith in authentic ways. We won't spend a ton of time on this here, but it is a theme that did arise in relation to calling in our conversations with our models of Christian faith and that we see implied in the work of all of them. We'll say more about the Christian community in chapter 5.

The theologian Miroslav Volf ties together the notion of calling with community when he argues that one of the purposes of meaningful work "is the flourishing of communities."

> We are communal beings. We live from community, and even the most "self-made" individual has been influenced by others. . . . And because we are such communal beings, we find the meaning of work in community. That community can be a family whose needs we seek to meet, a corporation for whose success we work, an ecclesiastical community to whose mission we want to contribute, a civic community whose vibrancy we strive to sustain, or even a world community.
>
> When we work for the well-being of communities, our work acquires a richer texture of meaning than

> when we work just for ourselves. We are then not only self-seeking; we are living for the benefit of others. And as we read in Scripture, "It is more blessed to give than to receive" (Acts 20:35). A faith that makes a difference nudges us to work out of love not just for ourselves but for our near and distant neighbors as well.[13]

Tessa's work with a refugee community illustrates this, and furthermore shows how her vision for an apparel company that created economic opportunities for refugee women developed directly out of living within and among that community. She didn't develop a sense of calling and then go find a community in which she could live out that calling; by living among the community first, she came to see the possibilities for purposeful work *in service to* that community. Tessa explains that, as she began working with a nonprofit ministry serving refugees and interacting more with the neighborhood and its inhabitants, she realized that she was very comfortable in that space even though it was a part of town that members of her own family wouldn't drive through. At the same time she was learning about John Perkins's work on Christian community development[14] and decided that if Jesus moved and worked among the poor and vulnerable, and if she called herself a follower of Jesus, then she too needed to live and work among the community she was feeling called to serve—so she moved into the neighborhood, where she lived for a few years before her work called her elsewhere.

In similar ways, each of our models of Christian faith live out their calling within community. Ron's work is about creating community and purpose for addicts who struggle to make it day after day without succumbing to their addiction. Paul's work with FOCUS Pittsburgh is specifically about love for and service to the community of broken individuals and providing hope and healing for that community. Julio's notion of "community" extends beyond boundaries of nation, creed, and color to welcome the stranger in

13. Volf, *Public Faith*, 33–34.

14. See the website of the Christian Community Development Association for more information: https://ccda.org/.

much the same way that God called the ancient Israelites to do. Emily strives in a difficult environment of partisan politics to find common ground between Republican and Democratic leaders to include environmental concerns in their agendas. And Rick works tirelessly to build community one relationship at a time between longtime adversaries in protracted conflicts around the world.

These people are *in it*, aren't they? Claiborne notes that far too many Christians "admire and worship Jesus without doing what he did," "applaud what he preached and stood for without caring about the same things," and "adore his cross without taking up ours."[15] The friends we've raised up as models are far from perfect, and they know it. But we believe they hold up to the light some attitudes and practices that reflect a genuine version of Christianity that makes it true and gives it credibility in this fractured and hurting world.

Conclusion

As we wrap up (for now, anyway) the topic of "embodied faith" and how our models live out their understanding of Christianity, let's return to the quotation by Mother Teresa at the start of the chapter: "You can find Calcutta anywhere in the world. You only need two eyes to see. Everywhere in the world there are people that are not loved, people that are not wanted nor desired, people that no one will help, people that are pushed away or forgotten. And this is the greatest poverty."

No one would question Mother Teresa's sense of divine calling—that her work in Calcutta and in other hurting places was her clear vocation. A person just does not do what she did without a seriously strong call to that life. She embodied the love of Christ for others, and we hold her up as a model of faith—a saint, in fact—to be emulated. But as Fr. Brian Kolodiejchuk explains in his collection of Mother Teresa's letters, she understood and experienced the notion of costly discipleship in becoming

15. Claiborne, *Irresistible Revolution*, 113.

discouraged and experiencing "the dark night of the soul" at many times—and sometimes for extended periods—in her life and work.[16]

Even despite her personal sacrifices and the realities of those dark and lonely periods, Mother Teresa knew she was called to her work. On a smaller scale—although no less important for being so—the models of Christian faith highlighted in this book have found their Calcutta too. God is calling each and every one of us to discover our unique Christian purpose and to respond by embodying active Christian love and sacrifice. We believe that is true and authentic discipleship indeed.

16. See Kolodiejchuk, *Mother Teresa*.

3

Depth of Faith, Breadth of Love

We must never forget that the only way we individually and collectively represent the kingdom of God is through loving, Christlike, sacrificial acts of service to others. Anything and everything else, however good and noble, lies outside the kingdom of God.

~ Greg Boyd, *The Myth of a Christian Nation*

I've held buckets . . . [for people] coming down off of heroin. . . . Why do I keep doing it? Oh my gosh, because you fall in love with them. These are women; they're moms, they're friends, they're sisters.

~ Tammy Beery

Introduction

The individuals we're focusing on in this book situate love at the center of what it means to be a Christian. You may be thinking, "Duh, everybody knows that love is central to Christianity" and therefore be tempted to skip this chapter. But we challenge you to stick with us through the next several pages because love *is* so central to Christianity, and we fear that most of us don't really reflect on what that means, what it looks like, and how the love Jesus introduced into the world two thousand years ago instituted a compassionate revolution. Focused, intentional love for all people, especially those whom our society seems to think are unlovable, is at the heart of what motivates the models of faith we emphasize in this book. We never tire of hearing their stories of embodied, radical love, and we think you'll find them fascinating too.

"They'll Know We Are Christians by Our Love"

You may be familiar with this old youth group/Christian campfire song. (And if it's stuck in your head for the rest of the day, we're really, really sorry.) But it is profoundly biblical in its simplicity: "They'll know we are Christians by our love, by our love / Yes they'll know we are Christians by our love." Jesus explained to his followers that their love for one another was how others would recognize them *as* his followers. In *The Ragamuffin Gospel*, author Brennan Manning makes the point: "Compassionate love is the axis of the Christian moral revolution and the only sign ever given by Jesus by which a disciple would be recognized."[1] And yet, look at how far Christians and the Christian faith more broadly fail at it. We love Greg Boyd's musing in relation to this, given the centrality of radical love to the ideals of authentic Christian faith: "One wonders why no one in church history has ever been considered a heretic for being unloving. People were anathematized [denounced or cast out] and often tortured and killed for disagreeing on matters of doctrine or on the authority of the church. But no one on record has ever been so much as rebuked for not loving as Christ loved."[2]

The idea of love is absolutely central to the biblical narrative. Like us, you are probably all too familiar with some of the ways that the Bible can be used to justify hatred, prejudice, and even violence. But we maintain that the arc of the Christian Scriptures

1. Manning, *Ragamuffin Gospel*, 153.

2. Boyd, *Myth of a Christian Nation*, 83.

is love, and any attempt to see or use it otherwise is a gross misunderstanding (at best) or a manipulation (at worst) of the story of Christianity. From the story of creation in Genesis to depictions of the *parousia*, or the second coming of Jesus, love is the core. There are lots of great books and articles about the various kinds of love mentioned in the Bible (*agape*, *philia*, etc.) and we encourage you to explore these concepts more; for our purposes here, however, a quick survey of the overarching centrality of love (between God and humans and between humans and humans) is a good reminder of the core of Christianity, as that core seems so lost on so many Christians.

So, at the risk of doing a total injustice to the biblical narrative by summarizing it in just a few short paragraphs . . .

As the story goes, in the beginning God creates in love. YHWH[3] makes all the components of the universe (sun, moon, stars, land and water, animals, vegetation), creates a human, sets that human up in a beautiful paradise, and then appears to realize (belatedly?) that it is not good for the human to be alone (Gen 2:18); out of love for that human and concern for his well-being, God makes a partner for the human to love and be loved by (Gen 2:21–23). Later in the Old Testament, divine love and concern drive the covenant relationship between YHWH and the people of Israel. Again and again, God comes to the aid of the Israelites, promising to protect and care for them[4] if they will only remain loyal and be good people who care for the orphan, the widow, and the stranger in the land (in other words, the most vulnerable and

3. "YHWH" (pronounced "Yah-weh") is understood as the sacred name of the God of the ancient Israelites, translated from Hebrew to Latin. Because the earliest Hebrew manuscripts only include the consonants, and out of respect for the Jewish tradition, which recognizes the name of God as sacred even in written and spoken form, we are following the scholarly convention of using "YHWH." Thanks to our friend John L. McLaughlin, professor of Old Testament/Hebrew Bible at the University of St. Michael's College in Toronto, for his assistance with this.

4. This way of interpreting the biblical narrative is known as "covenant history," as it understands the entire arc of the Bible to be about God's covenants with God's people, which culminates in the idea of the incarnation (God becoming human through Jesus) in the New Testament.

underprivileged).[5] Contrary to what many Christians think, the Old Testament prophets aren't called "prophets" because they foretold the future. Biblical prophecy was about interpreting the present, seeing all the ways humans were mucking it up by breaking God's commandments, taking advantage of the poor, and being unwelcoming to outsiders (among other things), and then being the ones to call people out on their crappy behavior. As you can imagine, they weren't exactly popular guys in ancient Israel. Their work was only futuristic in the sense that they were constantly saying, "Um, guys, if you don't pull it together and quit being total jerks, YHWH's coming back and it's not going to be pretty." Of course, the Israelites fail again and again to keep their end of the bargain, but God keeps coming back and remains faithful to God's promises—because, you know, God is God and doesn't *break* promises. This culminates in the ultimate act of love as understood by Christians: God becoming human through the person of Jesus Christ (the Incarnation) and sacrificing himself on behalf of all of us (idiots, every one) who can't manage to just be good, faithful people.

This brings us to Jesus, who for us is the core of all of it. Jesus claimed to fulfill the laws that God had given to God's people, not to abolish them (Matt 5:17). If we are unwilling to follow his teachings about radical love, then we misrepresent him as a liar to the rest of the world. What would be the sense in claiming to follow something we don't actually believe, let alone practice, and what motivation does that provide for the rest of the world to follow him? If we're not willing to take those teachings seriously—like *really* seriously—we might as well quit Christianity and let the whole idea drift away into history.[6]

5. Orphans, widows, and strangers in the land typically have a *really* tough time of it in current American culture. It was a gazillion times harder on those populations in ancient Israelite culture.

6. In the middle of drafting this chapter, a great article landed in Niki's inbox. It is worth a read for a short, powerful perspective on the importance of reclaiming Jesus's teachings for Christian life in our current historical moment in America: Giles, "Introducing Christians to Jesus."

Jesus exhibited a kind of love that his followers, his foes, and the broader Jewish community just hadn't known. In an environment with such intense social stratification based on gender, health, occupation, education, and other "accidental" factors of birth, Jesus touched the untouchables. He talked to people he had no business acknowledging, according to the ruling elites, let alone joining for a meal. Jesus lived the neighbor love he so often preached, and he extended the notion of "neighbor" to the stranger, the marginalized and downtrodden, and the enemy. This was radical in his day, and it's still radical in ours.

While time and space won't allow for an exhaustive survey, a couple of quick references to Jesus's teachings illustrate the kind of love to which he calls his followers. He tells the Pharisees (the elite in his society, and enforcers of Jewish law) which of God's commandments is the most important: "You shall love the Lord your God with all your heart, and with all your soul, and with all your mind.' This is the greatest and first commandment. And a second is like it: 'You shall love your neighbor as yourself.' On these two commandments hang all the law and the prophets" (Matt 22:34–40). In other words, says Jesus, love comes first. The rest of it—the specifics of how we are to behave in society and organize our lives together—needs to be in line with the ultimate law of love.

In Jesus's famous parable of the Good Samaritan, in which a man is robbed and beaten, left for dead, passed over by two members of his own community, and eventually rescued by a Samaritan man, Jesus turns convention on its head by making the Samaritan—a member of a neighboring community despised by the Jews—the hero of the story. Echoes of this story abound in the work of later New Testament writers, as the fledgling Christian community was trying to find its way and make sense of Jesus's teachings: "Those who say, 'I love God,' and hate their brothers or sisters, are liars; for those who do not love a brother or sister whom they have seen, cannot love God whom we have not seen" (1 John 4:20).[7]

7. When the New Testament refers to "brothers and sisters," it almost always means members of the community—not actual siblings.

When we talk about the "revolutionary" aspect of Jesus's understanding of neighbor love, we aren't kidding. It's difficult to overemphasize just how profound Christianity's radical new notion of love was. Prior to Christianity, Greek thought had influenced the cultures of the region, including Jewish culture. In Greek-influenced civilization, humans were not equal. Some were born at the top of the social order and others at the bottom, and this social stratification was accepted as reality.[8] This stratification was part of the cosmic order. Christianity shattered this idea in claiming a personal God (not an impersonal, static "cosmic order") and in insisting that God saw and loved all humans as equals. Timothy Keller points out that "for the Greeks, the claim that the 'universal cosmic order' could be identified with an individual was 'insanity.' For Christians, however, it meant a radical 'personalizing' of the universe. It was the unprecedented idea that the power behind the world was love, a personal God."[9] Keller adds, "For the first time the supreme goal of life was not self-control and rationality but love. Love was required to redirect the human person away from self-centeredness toward serving God and others."[10]

Although *love* is a word people throw around a lot and seems, on the face of it, like a concept we can all get behind, when we really think about what it means in practice from a biblical standpoint, it can be a little (okay, a lot) overwhelming. "Exaggeration and overstatement are not the danger here. The danger lurks in our subtle attempts to rationalize our moderation in this regard. Turning the other cheek, walking the extra mile, offering no resistance to injury, and forgiving seventy times seven are not whims of the Son of Man."[11] This is wildly challenging. But going back to some of the things we argued in the previous chapter: if

8. Ferry, *Brief History of Thought*, 72.

9. Keller, *Making Sense of God*, 46.

10. Keller, *Making Sense of God*, 45. It is worth noting that these Christian ideas are the early foundations for later developments toward the notion of modern "human rights." See Ferry, *Brief History of Thought*, especially chapter 3, "The Victory of Christianity over Greek Philosophy," 55–91.

11. Manning, *Ragamuffin Gospel*, 153.

the Christian community—and the love that is supposed to be so central to that community—looks too much like the rest of the world, then what's the point? Authentic, biblical, Christian love isn't half-baked, convenient, or limited to those who look and think like us. Christians are called to something far bigger and, frankly, far more difficult. But don't we *want* to expect something more? Don't we expect to be challenged to love radically, to love in an embodied way that radically clashes with the sort of love expected and practiced by the world? The part that gets us is knowing that some of our readers will balk at the notion of "radical" love—the thing is, however, is that it's not radical: it's just biblical. We're called to an embodied, compassionate, active love of all people, even—especially—those whom society casts aside. Failure to heed the call to love *means we're not actually doing Christianity at all*!

Christians and Love: Some Crappy News

We think it is fair to say that we Christians as a whole fail pretty miserably to live out the radical, countercultural love ethic that Jesus asked of anyone who claimed to follow him. (And please recall that we include ourselves in that assessment—we readily admit that we, too, are pretty crappy Christians.) As one study noted, non-Christians do not think Christians live up to the call to love all people. According to a study by the Barna Group, 85 percent of people outside the faith saw Christians as "hypocritical" (and a whopping 47 percent of young people *inside* the faith felt that way about Christianity!).[12] And 87 percent of outsiders and 53 percent of young Christians saw Christians in general as being judgmental. Apparently, the image of the crappy Christian abounds, leaving little room for people to see Christ's compassionate love and care as markers of Christian faith.

Tony Campolo, an evangelical pastor known (and often criticized) for his inclusive love ethic, gets at this in an anecdote he tells regularly to his large audiences: "I have three things I'd like

12. Kinnamon and Lyons, *UnChristian*, 40.

to say today. . . . First, while you were sleeping last night, 30,000 kids died of starvation or diseases related to malnutrition. Second, most of you don't give a s—. What's worse is that you're more upset with the fact that I said 's—' than the fact that 30,000 kids died last night."[13] Ron, our friend who works with recovering addicts, reflects the spirit of Campolo's words: "Do I cuss? Of course I cuss. . . . I have a hard enough time loving my neighbor. I think that's part of what's wrong with Christianity—we get focused on all these check-off lists."

If Christians really are that hypocritical, judgmental, and unloving (and our own experience would lead us to believe that the Barna study is pretty spot on), this has some serious repercussions. It means that it will be difficult to convince non-Christians that Christians should be taken seriously, let alone that they should become one. It also means that we shouldn't be surprised when Christians who have a good understanding of authentic Christianity decide to leave the church when they experience that hypocrisy and judgment. This came through clearly in conversations with the models of faith highlighted here. Recall from chapter 1 that Ron left his church after encountering some crappy Christians there. Tessa struggled within her church to hear a message of what Christians should do (love and serve others) rather than a list of things that Christians shouldn't do (premarital sex, drug use, etc.); it was a "ticket out of hell," as she put it, rather than a gateway to a rewarding life based on loving others. Julio struggles to understand why his fellow Christians scratch their heads at his very strong call to love and serve those whom society deems worthless. And so on.

However, that crappy news is not the end of the story. Ron's faith in Christianity was eventually restored at Sugartree Ministries. He was inspired by the local church people who were volunteering their time and serving meals. Although his first impression was "why would they waste all their time to come here and serve these people," as weeks passed, he realized these were "very sweet people" serving the community. They were authentic Christians

13. Quoted in Olsen, "Positive Prophet," 34.

living out their faith for those on the margins of society, not judgmental, selfish Christians: "People trying to love people—it's what drew me [back to the church]."

Tessa's journey didn't involve leaving the church altogether at any point, but it did involve a major shift in her understanding of what the Christian life is really supposed to be about. That shift occurred in part after finding a more love-based, encouraging church as well as reading John Perkins, John Piper, and other inspirational authors. Perkins cofounded the Christian Community Development Association (CCDA), which aims "to inspire, train, and connect Christians who seek to bear witness to the Kingdom of God by reclaiming and restoring under-resourced communities."[14] Tessa began to wonder why she hadn't learned about such concepts in church and why all Christians were not engaged in this sort of work. Piper's work challenged her from a different but related angle. Piper urges Christians to let go of the American Dream's pursuit of trivial material goods and live a life focused on radical love of others. Piper contrasts two stories of people nearing the end of their lives. The first story is of two eighty-year-old women: one a missionary, one a doctor. While serving in Africa, both are killed instantly in a car crash when their brakes give out. In the second story, Piper describes a couple who retire in their fifties and move to Florida. They spend their time collecting sea shells and cruising on their boat. In Piper's rendering, he asks his congregation which story is more tragic. When the congregation answers that the first story is more tragic, he asks how impressed God will be with a shell collection. For Piper, the tragedy is that we are convinced by our culture that we should spend our lives focusing on the wrong goals. In Piper's view, "That is a tragedy. And people today are spending billions of dollars to persuade you to embrace that tragic dream. Over against that, I put my protest: Don't buy it. Don't waste your life."[15] Tessa took the hard-hitting

14. See the Christian Community Development Association, https://ccda.org/.

15. Piper, *Don't Waste Your Life*, 46.

cue, made a radical change to her career plans, and chose a path of service to and love of her refugee neighbors.

While the hypocrisy of the church has never driven Julio away, he has been unable to find a church that is generally on the same page with him about his Christian values and ethical concerns. In addition, he faces constant questioning by fellow Christians as he works on issues of immigration reform and direct service to migrants. When Julio uses social media to advocate for compassion toward immigrants, he is often criticized harshly by other Christians. For Julio, taking Jesus seriously means he must continue to fight on behalf of the "stranger in the land," but he must do so in love. As a result, Julio will respond with something like: "As a Christian, I'm praying that God may touch your heart, and that you start seeing people as human beings with dignity." Of course, this rarely changes the views of the person on the other end, but it is the right way to respond *and* very often changes the tone of the conversation.

What we find most compelling and most important for the purposes of this book is that for our models, as faith has deepened, their capacity to love more broadly across political, racial, ethnic, class, national, and religious lines and boundaries has grown and widened. That, for us, is the heart of this chapter: depth of faith leads to breadth of love. More specifically, a deep and abiding sense that Jesus is not a liar and really means what he says leads quite clearly and quite simply to an unfettered capacity to love our neighbors: our poor neighbors, our refugee and immigrant neighbors, our drug-addicted neighbors, our Muslim and Jewish and atheist and Hindu neighbors, our white and black and brown neighbors, our Republican and Democrat and independent and apolitical neighbors.

So we need to dig in. We need to look to the Scriptures of our tradition with fresh eyes to see the arc of love that exists there. We need to focus on what Jesus said and did, and what the early church taught and lived out in the wake of his death, all couched in the social, political, and religious context of Jesus's day so that we can better translate those teachings and actions for our own time.

So What *Should* Christian Love Look Like?

Sometimes the Christian Scriptures can seem confusing, especially at first glance. And some parts seem downright impossible to wrestle with and attempt to understand. But Jesus doesn't get much clearer in identifying directly with the poor, the marginalized, and the societal outcast than in Matthew 25. Jesus doesn't just call his followers to feed the hungry, welcome the stranger, clothe the naked, and visit the imprisoned—he says that when Christians do these things, they do it *to him*. How much clearer can he get on this point? But what does that look like? Does donating food or clothing at the local homeless shelter or mailing a check to a charitable organization satisfy Jesus's teachings? These are good, maybe even great, things to do, but we figure there's more to it. Shane Claiborne puts it this way:

> We can volunteer in a social program or distribute excess food and clothing through organizations and never have to open up our homes, our beds, our dinner tables. When we get to heaven, we will be separated into those sheep and goats Jesus talks about in Matthew 25 based on how we cared for the least among us. I'm just not convinced that Jesus is going to say, "When I was hungry, you gave a check to the United Way and they fed me," or, "When I was naked, you donated clothes to the Salvation Army and they clothed me." Jesus is not seeking distant acts of charity. He seeks concrete acts of love: "you fed me . . . you visited me in prison . . . you welcomed me into your home . . . you clothed me" . . .
>
> When the church becomes a place of brokerage rather than an organic community, she ceases to be alive. She ceases to be something we are, the living bride of Christ. The church becomes a distribution center, a place where the poor come to get stuff and the rich come to dump stuff. Both go away satisfied (the rich feel good, the poor get clothed and fed), but no one leaves transformed. No radical new community is formed. And Jesus did not set up a program but modeled a way of living that incarnated the reign of God. . . . That reign did not spread through organizational establishments or structural

> systems. It spread like disease—through touch, through breath, through life. It spread through people infected by love.[16]

Our models provide us with some examples of this "more" which, as we discussed in the previous chapter, almost always involves sacrifice. Rick gave up a six-figure salary in horse racing to join Christian Peacemaker Teams and live in war zones for about $200 per month. Tessa quit her plans in an industry that she felt didn't align with her sense of Christian calling. Tammy holds the bucket while women vomit as they come off of heroin. Julio and Emily deal constantly with the frustration of trying to change public policies that harm people and the environment.

So, fair warning—Christian love may make you look a little odd. You may do things that seem to the world to be irrational. And some of those acts may fail, but it is important to remember that Jesus calls us to be faithful, to follow our vocation. Some measure of worldly success may accompany following your call, but worldly success is never the end goal.

The Transformative Power of Loving Our Enemies

Our focus so far in this chapter has really been on love of the marginalized in society and the need for Christians to start acting like better Christians through active, embodied love. That really should be the easy part, so it's shocking that so few Christians manage to practice *that* kind of love. But what about loving our enemies, which was also on Jesus's teaching agenda? At times over the last two thousand years, and in places throughout the world, Christians have transformed oppressive conditions, conflicts, and other crappy situations by choosing love over hatred. That has often taken the form of active nonviolence, which involves the refusal to hurt people, even those inflicting harm, in the interest of changing the situation. Nonviolence refuses to see violence as a proper means to any end, choosing instead to transform a

16. Claiborne, *Irresistible Revolution*, 158–59.

situation by breaking the cycle of violence. In his sermon "Loving Your Enemies," Martin Luther King Jr. said,

> To our most bitter opponents we say: "We shall match your capacity to inflict suffering by our capacity to endure suffering. We shall meet your physical force with soul force. Do to us what you will, and we shall continue to love you. We cannot in all good conscience obey your unjust laws, because non-co-operation [*sic*] with evil is as much a moral obligation as is co-operation [*sic*] with good. Throw us in jail, and we shall still love you. Send your hooded perpetrators of violence into our community at the midnight hour and beat us and leave us half dead, and we shall still love you. But be ye assured that we will wear you down by our capacity to suffer. One day we shall win freedom, but not only for ourselves. We shall so appeal to your heart and conscience that we shall win *you* in the process, and our victory will be a double victory."[17]

King, like so many other well-known models of authentic Christian faith (William Wilberforce, Dorothy Day, Cesar Chavez, Rosa Parks, and James Lawson, to name a few), used the Christian ideal of enemy love for the very practical purpose of transforming oppressive social and political realities. Odd, isn't it, that Christians around the world look to individual Christians such as these as saints, yet we are so reluctant to practice this ideal and put it to good practical use in our own situations?

Critics of nonviolence tend to be people who know very little about it as a strategic maneuver. (We know something about this, as we have taught, written about, and practiced nonviolence ourselves and have heard *all* the criticism.) Learning to practice a love-based ethic of nonviolence takes investment of time, energy, and other resources. We and others would contend that nonviolent love even of our enemies, as a response to conflict, aligns best with the teachings of Jesus. And it's not just what Jesus teaches—it actually works! It works because it alters the system that allows one group to oppress another. An identifying mark of King's Christian

17. King, *Strength to Love*, 54–55.

nonviolence was his concern for the oppressor. He wanted to work nonviolently with the oppressor in ending oppression altogether. King believed the one who oppresses is not actually free himself; he is controlled by prejudice and hate, and being controlled by anything is not freedom. King was not interested in turning the oppressor into the newly oppressed, or "winning" or beating the enemy. This was evident at the end of the Nashville lunch counter sit-ins and store boycotts aimed at undoing segregation in the 1960s. When it became clear that segregation policies were going to end—that King and his supporters had indeed "won"—there was no victory dance or humiliation of store owners. Instead, King and his supporters quietly ended the boycott without public announcements. To us, that is creative, Jesus-inspired Christian love of enemy or opponent. It is embodied and transformative love.

Enemy Love: A Few Inspiring Stories

At this point, you may be thinking, "Martin Luther King Jr. and his associates might have used nonviolent, Christian love to make some big changes, but I'm no MLK." We totally get that, because neither are we. Again, that's the point of the book—highlighting ways in which regular folks in their regular lives can live their Christian values faithfully, which means lovingly and sacrificially and a lot of other positive adverbs. That said, we want to share just a couple of dramatic stories from our models of Christian faith—because those stories are incredibly inspiring and, frankly, cool stories to tell.

Paul's stint in the US Army during the war in Iraq provides our first story of embodied, other-centered love. A few weeks into the war, Paul could see the toll of war and the escalating tensions between his fellow worn-out soldiers and Iraqis who were fearful, angry, and frustrated by a lack of electricity and clean water. An "us vs. them" mentality was beginning to take hold among the soldiers. The latent conflict erupted one day when a Muslim Iraqi boy who had been hired to paint the barracks noticed that one of the soldiers was using a Muslim prayer rug to wipe dust and dirt from his boots. The boy picked up the rug, and in an emotionally charged plea to Paul, begged to purchase the rug to prevent further disrespect to his religious tradition. Paul knew this wasn't a simple decision to make. It could certainly lead to trouble with the soldier if he gave or sold property to the "enemy" without permission. He could tell the kid to get lost, but Paul could see how important this was to him. He chose to give the boy the rug and later reimbursed the soldier. Afterward he took flak from his fellow soldiers for appeasing the kid—the "enemy," in their eyes—but Paul was moved to rise above those categories and do the loving thing even in the middle of a war, and even for someone who didn't share his religious perspective.

The next story involves our friend Rick and occurs in 2002 in Hebron, Palestine. Recall that Rick works for Christian Peacemaker Teams, which sends teams of peacemakers into areas of conflict to engage in relational, on-the-ground peacemaking—and occasionally, to engage in direct action in a volatile situation. One afternoon, Rick received a phone call from the principal of a local Palestinian elementary school. He could barely hear the principal over the sound of children screaming in the background, but managed to hear him tell Rick to come quickly to the school because Israeli soldiers were teargassing it and the children were trapped inside. Grabbing a raw onion (onions can be rubbed under the eyes to prevent the more harmful effects of tear gas, and Rick had been down the tear-gas road before), Rick ran out the door and started making phone calls along the way: first to fellow CPTers for backup, and then to Israeli military leaders he knew who might be willing to contact the troop commander at the school and call off whatever was happening there.

As he approached the school, Rick saw children and teachers hanging out of the windows, screaming and choking on tear gas—and a line of Israeli soldiers guarding the school gate. At the gate, the assistant principal was arguing with the commander, whose rifle was pointed in his chest. The commander claimed that kids from the school had thrown rocks at the soldiers the day before, so the soldiers were punishing them. Behind the principal were children and teachers trying to push their way out, but the troops were blocking the exit. Realizing that the commander was the key to releasing the children, and that the shouting match between the assistant principal and commander could escalate, Rick slid in between the commander's gun and the assistant principal—and now the gun was in Rick's chest. Despite years of training to remain calm in such situations, Rick could feel his anger rising as the screams of the children continued, and he too began to argue heatedly with the commander for their release.

At that point, Rick's cell phone rang. Thinking it might be a military leader who might be able to help, Rick answered: "Yeah, this is Rick." It wasn't a military leader; it was Rick's friend "Crazy George," an outgoing, fun-loving Palestinian who's always upbeat and positive. "Hey man, what's happening?" said George pleasantly. George's friendly greeting immediately brought Rick back to his own human center, where he could see the humanity even of the man shouting at him with a gun in his ribs. Thinking quickly and creatively, as he'd been trained for years to do, he held the phone out to the commander: "Here, it's for you. It's your mom."

"That's not my mom," said the commander, visibly taken aback. Holding the phone out further, Rick insisted, "Yes it is, it's your mom."

"That's not my mom," argued the commander, taking a step away from Rick.

"It is your mom, and she wants to know what you're doing right now."

In a moment, the commander had drawn his soldiers away from the school and the children and teachers were free to leave and attend to the nasty effects of the tear gas. Weeks later, Rick learned that the commander's mother was an Israeli elementary school teacher; Rick surmises that the fake phone call forced the commander to consider how he'd feel if it was his mother and her students being harmed.

This story conveys the willingness of Rick to put his own life on the line out of his love for Palestinian children and teachers, most of whom he didn't even know. In this instance, too, nonviolence stands against any criticism of it as a "weak" or soft response to violent assault: it can "do what laws and bullets and bombs can never do—namely, bring about transformation in an enemy's heart."[18] We'll share another story from Rick's experience in chapter 5, where we include it because of its connection to the idea of participation in God's redemptive work in the world; the point of telling the story about the school and Paul's story above is to demonstrate how we are called to love enemies, regardless of what others think, and to demonstrate the transformative nature of enemy love.

So What?

We know, we know. Most of us can't identity with the stories of Paul and Rick described above. Most of us will never be in such dramatic situations, and we're not asking the reader to go out and find drama. But certainly we can learn from these stories and take the love-centered Christian courage that Paul and Rick exemplified and apply it to all the little challenges and battles that pop up in our daily lives. Julio models this in how he deals with his critics and their animosity on social media. Tammy responded directly to the needs she saw in her own community. Ron works to bring healing and hope to people whom our society would just as well throw away. Emily works across political party lines to develop goodwill and relationships, patiently nurturing concern for environmental policies that are in the best interest of all humans. Tessa chooses to employ a local population that would otherwise struggle to make a living for their families. And both Rick and Paul live out their commitments to a broad, borderless Christian love in their day-to-day lives and work.

"The kingdom of God does not seek to conquer; it seeks to transform," argues Greg Boyd in *The Myth of a Christian Nation*.[19] Of course this is true—never does Jesus tell his followers that they

18. Boyd, *Myth of a Christian Nation*, 32.

19. Boyd, *Myth of a Christian Nation*, 179.

need to try to control the political realm or otherwise seek power. Everything was about relationships, and community, and turning systems of oppression and unfairness on their heads, and changing hearts through active, transformative love. Our work as people of faith, people who claim the adjective "Christian," must begin to focus collectively on practicing that "radical" (no, *biblical*!) love-based ethic of inclusive love. And it has to be an active, sacrificial love that goes beyond sentimentality to result in true social change. We simply cannot, with any integrity, claim loyalty to Jesus and his teachings if this kind of love is not at the center.

Speaking of loyalty: the notion of following Jesus and remaining loyal to his teachings has other implications for how to avoid being a crappy Christian. We turn to this notion of competing loyalties in the next chapter.

4

Identities and Loyalties

Truth is, many in the American church are Americans first and Christians second. They have never consciously prioritized these loyalties, though, because it has never occurred to them there may be a difference, let alone a conflict, between the two. But when American patriotism is blended with Christian spirituality, the former will always bully the latter. . . . Do not misunderstand me: I am grateful for the ways God has blessed America, and I believe we should express our citizenship by helping to order society according to the will of God as we understand it. But letting God define political commitments is one thing; letting political commitments define God is entirely something else. Unfortunately, the powerful pull of politics too often trivializes God into a god-of-my-nation unable to do much more than offer a misty-eyed sentimentalism.

~ Donald W. McCullough, *The Trivialization of God*

But you have to remember, God is your King; you may have a president, but God is your King!

~ Ron Cordy

Introduction

In the last chapter, we asked you to stick with us through what you might have thought was a "no-brainer" chapter on Christian love. In this chapter, we're asking you to stick with us through a discussion of the thing that divides American Christians more than anything else in the current historical moment (and honestly, probably at all times): politics. To be clear, we're not interested here in partisan politics—Republicans vs. Democrats, liberals vs. conservatives, voting patterns and habits, and the like—but rather politics as it pertains to issues of patriotic identity and allegiances and what it means for Christians in America to order their allegiances correctly. In other words, how do we begin to consider what a *Christ-centered* politics might look like?

This will likely be the most challenging chapter in the book for most of our readers, as it asks American Christians to reflect deeply and critically on what it means to identify as a Christian even as we recognize ourselves as citizens of a particular nation. What do we do when the claims of our faith conflict, sometimes severely, with the claims of our nation? We understand this is a very difficult subject. But the very fact that people get so upset when challenged to see their political views through a Christian lens is indicative of the reality that too many of us prioritize our politics above the tenets of our faith—often entirely unconsciously. Sometimes, we discover that we've conflated the two, which is equally problematic and which we'll discuss more in depth a bit later. We argue in this chapter that getting our allegiances right is absolutely critical to avoiding the crappy Christian trap. Our models of faith share a sense of rightly ordered allegiance even as they represent a wide variety of political views and affiliations. Before we get to that, however, we need to spend a little time exploring some concepts and historical background.

Patriotism, Nationalism, and Other Complex Issues

Unpacking Some Definitions

Standing at a sporting event to sing the national anthem, saying the Pledge of Allegiance in a school classroom, wearing a flag pin on our lapel—we see or do these things often and don't question them. They strike us as positive things. They make us feel like we're part of a group, joining us to others through a shared sense of national identity. This collective identity connects us to people with whom we presume to share some similar political ideals and values. It makes us feel good about those values and where we live and, by extension, who we are. We get these same feelings when we cheer for our country during the Olympics or when we feel inspired to donate money or blood to people we don't even know following a natural disaster.

What we call these allegiances or identities is debated, but the terms that are often used are *patriotism* or sometimes *nationalism*. These two terms are sometimes used interchangeably, and there is no universally agreed-upon definition for either. However, in this book, we follow the lead of many scholars who describe patriotism as a more positive love of country that gets to the kinds of feelings described above and nationalism as a far more dangerous perspective for Christians.

Before he worked with Christian Peacemaker Teams, Rick led groups to provide help in post-natural disaster situations and talks about patriotism as being "good if it is bringing people together for the betterment of all." Importantly, this type of patriotic love of country often includes critique based on that love and the desire to see one's country live up to its values. Nationalism, in contrast, often leads to seeing one's country as better than other countries: "Patriotism researchers have reached some (although far from uniform) consensus that a sense of superiority and need for foreign dominance better reflect nationalism than patriotism."[1]

1. Huddy and Khatib, "American Patriotism, National Identity," 63.

For us, from a Christian perspective, it matters less what term is used to describe these feelings and more that we properly order our identities and allegiances. We need to ask to whom or what we will give our allegiance. Drawing from our last chapter, we must be careful that our devotion to country does not interfere with the Christian call to authentic and selfless love of *all* people. More directly: we need to consider whether our patriotism limits our love. Does it exclude certain populations within our borders, or our neighbors beyond those borders? Many Christians, including each of our models of faith highlighted in this book, are concerned about the ways in which healthy patriotism can devolve into unhealthy, uncritical patriotic allegiance and even dangerous forms of nationalism which pit America against other nations and create an "America first" mentality.

Let us be clear: we firmly believe there is no room for this way of thinking for those who take a biblical, Jesus-centered approach to Christianity. Unfortunately, American Christianity is rife with people and whole congregations who put country before God and neighbor. Michael Budde puts the situation in stark terms:

> Few people inside the churches seem eager to admit it, but in matters of human allegiance, loyalty, and priorities, Christianity is a nearly complete, unabashed failure. It has had little discernible impact in making the Sermon on the Mount (Pope John Paul II's "magna charta of Gospel morality") remotely relevant in Christian life and lifestyles; it has provided no alternative sense of community capable of withstanding the absolutist claims of state, movement, and market. . . .
>
> The failures are so huge, the contradictions with the gospel so enormous, that they don't even register as subjects of concern in the churches.[2]

We think Budde is spot on. And we're here to register our concern. We do so not as non-patriots or America-haters but as people who are patriotic enough to want our country to do more, to be better. In the same way that our love for our children compels us

2. Budde, *Church as Counterculture*, 214.

to call out their bad behavior so that they will grow into good, loving, wise adults, so too our love for our country compels us to engagement with and critique of our government's actions and policies, both at home and abroad.

Dietrich Bonhoeffer, Dorothy Day, Óscar Romero, Martin Luther King Jr., William Wilberforce, and scores of other Christian social changemakers throughout history have understood the critical need to properly order their allegiances, living out their loyalty to Christ over the state. The state worked to suppress their voices and, in many cases, even killed those whose loyalty to Jesus got in the way of the state's agenda. American Christians have always needed to differentiate loyalties, which we'll discuss further below. We believe that this is especially important right now.

Allegiances and Loyalties: A Quick and Dirty History of Church and State

As we noted earlier in the book, if we fail to understand the historical moment into which Jesus was born, carried out his ministry, and was crucified, we will fail to comprehend the meaning of his message and the compassionate revolutionary power behind that message. We have to begin in the first century CE, in a tiny backwater region called Palestine. This was the era known as the Pax Romana, or "Roman Peace." The Roman Empire controlled almost all of the regions around the Mediterranean Sea. As long as you behaved and complied, as the majority of the Jews in Palestine did, you were allowed to mostly carry on with your life, but you had to pay taxes to the overlords, and you still knew you weren't *free*. In Palestine, there were the Jewish groups with relative power who were sort of suck-ups to the Roman government (like the Sadducees and the Pharisees—remember those guys from your Sunday school class?), and then there were Jewish groups like the Zealots who were the freedom fighters of first-century Palestine and absolutely hated their Roman rulers.

Into this sociopolitical situation Jesus is born. He "comforts the afflicted and afflicts the comfortable," is eventually crucified by the Romans for threatening the standing sociopolitical order, and up pops the church. Members of the Christian "Way" (the term the early Christians used before there were buildings and hierarchies in an institution called "the church") suddenly needed to figure out how to order their lives and community based on what they had learned from their Messiah, all the while being persecuted by the pagan Roman Empire.

It is so important to understand what the early Christians were doing. They stood against the state so radically that they were often persecuted for it. And why were they persecuted? First, they were just *weird* in the eyes of their overlords: they worshiped a traitor to the state who had been put to death in the most heinous way ("Treason!" charged the outsiders); they held "love feasts" and secret meetings under cover of darkness ("Dirty, perverted Christians!" alleged the outsiders); and in celebrating Eucharist (or communion, or the Lord's Supper, depending on your Christian affiliation), they claimed to consume the body and blood of their leader ("Ew, cannibalism!" declared the outsiders). But a bigger issue for the empire was Christian disdain for Roman religion and its deities and Christian refusal to pledge allegiance to the emperor, who had set himself up as a god.[3] It was the ultimate conflict between Christians' religious sensibilities and what the state asked of them. And how did they answer? *They literally would rather have died* than cave on their Christian convictions

3. For a more thorough but accessible history of the early church and its context, see chapter 1, "The Beginning of the Story," in John Drane's *Introducing the New Testament*, 9–45. Drane quotes from early writings about the Christians: "The Christians form among themselves secret societies that exist outside the system of laws . . . an obscure and mysterious community founded on revolt and on the advantage that accrues from it . . . They form a rabble of profane conspiracy. Their alliance consists in meetings at night with solemn rituals and inhuman revelries . . . They despise temples as if they were tombs. They disparage the gods and ridicule our sacred rites . . . Just like a rank growth of weeds, the abominable haunts where this impious confederacy meet are multiplying all over the world . . . To venerate an executed criminal and . . . the wooden cross on which he was executed is to erect altars which befit lost and depraved wretches. (Origen, *Cels.* 8.17; 3.14; Minucius Felix, *Oct.* 8.4; 9.1–6)." Drane, *New Testament*, 14.

of communal love and loyalty to Jesus. The Roman government responded by murdering them: "The root of the word allegiance means 'Lord'; that's exactly what the early Christians were executed for, for pledging an allegiance to another kingdom, another Lord—treason."[4]

Despite their persecution—maybe, as some Christian theologians have argued, *because* of it—Christians formed a strong alternative community. They largely refused to participate in the Roman military, because doing so meant that they would necessarily be pledging allegiance to Caesar and thus to the empire. And if you read the book of Acts in the Bible, you will learn how tightly knit this community was, even going so far as to participate in radical sharing: "There was not a needy person among them, for as many as owned lands or houses sold them and brought the proceeds of what was sold. They laid it at the apostles' feet, and it was distributed to each as any had need" (Acts 4:34–35). In forming such alternative communities with alternative loyalties, early Christians were accused of "turning the world upside down" and "acting contrary to the decrees of the emperor, saying that there is another king named Jesus" (Acts 17:6–7).

If you're a Christian living in early twenty-first-century America, you may be looking around and thinking, "Uh. Yeah. Christianity looks *nothing* like that."[5] If so, you may also be starting to understand why some Christians, even patriotic ones, are so wary of the dangers of uber-patriotism, which can devolve into idolizing the nation and even its symbols, such as the flag, the Constitution, and the national anthem. So what happened? How did we get to where we are today, where American Christianity as a whole looks so little like the earliest Christian communities?

With sincere apologies to all the historians, here goes seventeen hundred years' worth of church history in one paragraph: in 311 CE, the Roman Emperor Constantine decided he sort of liked Christianity—or was at least savvy enough to know that he needed something to unify the empire. Within a few years,

4. Claiborne, *Irresistible Revolution*, 194.

5. Once again, that's why we've written this book!

he declared Christianity the official religion of the empire. Quite suddenly, Christianity went from being a persecuted minority to the powerful majority. The good news was that Christians were no longer in real danger of being murdered for their faith. The bad news, though, was that Christians were no longer in danger of being murdered for their faith. You see, when Constantine made Christianity the official religion, opportunistic people who had just yesterday hated Christians, since that was the "in" thing to do, suddenly realized that good jobs and other privileges came with being a Christian. There went the purity of the church: for every Tom, Dick, and Harry (okay, it's fourth-century Rome, so every Titus, Dominicus, and Halius) who joined up, another measure of inauthentic Christianity was added into what had once been the true community of Christ. And once you have a watered-down church, a compromising shift in attitudes in the other direction by Christians toward the state is easier. Rodney Clapp summarizes this shift: "With Constantine, Christian history begins to be told as the story of dynasties. . . . The question is no longer 'How can we survive and remain faithful Christians under Caesar?' but becomes 'How can we adjust the church's expectations so that Caesar can consider himself a faithful Christian?'"[6] In other words, Christians initially asked how they could faithfully follow Jesus and survive under a repressive government, the values of which had nothing to do with Christian values of love, mercy, sharing, nonviolence, and radical loyalty to Jesus and the body of Christ. But once the Roman Empire became Christianized, Christians asked themselves to what degree they would water down their early beliefs so that Caesar could be considered a Christian. Incidentally, this new relationship would eventually lead to Christians joining the military and fighting on behalf of the empire. You can see the uncomfortable balancing act that comes into sharp focus here. And Christianity, at various times and to varying degrees in its various forms all over the world, has been working to compromise between two masters ever since. The rest, as they say, is history.

6. Clapp, *Peculiar People*, 26.

The Case against Nationalism for People Called "Christians"

So now we begin to wade into some really treacherous waters: a critique of nationalism as incompatible with loyalty to Jesus. We're aware that a few of our readers are going to slam the book closed right here, throw it across the room, and holler, "Treason!" Or, for the more theologically inclined readers, maybe we'll get, "Blasphemers!"

For those of you who are still reading, the fact that some of your fellow readers just did that is at the heart of the issue: too many American Christians equate loyalty to the nation with loyalty to their Christian faith. These are not the same, and failure to see that is the real blasphemy. American nationalism—uncritical loyalty to the United States (exemplified through devotion to things such as the flag, the national anthem, the Constitution, the government, or any other symbol or function of this country)—has become a religion unto itself. Too many Christians' behaviors and language reveal their idolatry of the nation over loyalty and commitment to Jesus and his teachings. And in addition to the sin of idolatry, nationalism flies in the face of Jesus's call to neighbor love, including our global neighbors. As we argued in the previous chapter, we are called to love those beyond human-made borders—as they, too, are made in God's image.

We could spend pages discussing all the ways that nationalism has been bad for the world and has put Christianity on the wrong side of history. Perhaps just a couple of quick examples will suffice. It was the national arrogance of the "Christian" western European powers, coupled with their greed, that led them to colonize other parts of the world, enslaving, exploiting, or exterminating people in other nations for centuries. Nationalism enabled Hitler to rally the German people (a majority of them Christian) to comply with increasing antagonism against Jews and foreigners, an antagonism that finally culminated in the Holocaust. And as the United States prepared to invade Iraq in 2003, some American Christians pointed out that this would mean bombing a country that contained over a million Christians. Did you hear *your* pastor or priest talking about the problem of killing our brothers and sisters in Christ juxtaposed against the call to support our country's war effort? Yeah. Neither did we.

In his 2005 book, *The Myth of a Christian Nation: How the Quest for Political Power Is Destroying the Church*, Gregory Boyd argues bluntly, "My thesis . . . is this: I believe a significant segment of American evangelicalism is guilty of nationalistic and political idolatry."[7] Again, we know people might be tempted to slam the book shut right here and chuck it in the trash. (Hey, at least recycle it rather than sending it to a landfill, okay?) To be fair, it's not just American evangelicalism, either. It's also American Catholicism and American mainline Protestant churches and lots of other denominations and sects within Christianity that succumb to this same temptation. Boyd's charge of idolatry is hard to hear if you're a Christian living in the United States today. But is he wrong? We would say, frankly: no. The Bible itself warns against serving two masters; a person with two masters "will either hate the one and love the other, or be devoted to the one and despise the other" (Matt 6:24). When our national allegiance (and identity as "Americans") becomes the priority over allegiance to Christ (and identity as "Christians"), we might as well just be truthful and stop calling ourselves Christ-followers, or Christians.

We hope it is becoming clearer why some Christians have an aversion to nationalism and to the unhealthy forms of patriotism that can be the slippery slope to it. These are not people who hate their country or who are ungrateful for their nation or their freedoms or rights. In fact, it is quite the opposite—they are people who deeply love their country. Ron, our friend who works with addicts, puts it this way:

> I'm a very patriotic dude. . . . Jesus said render unto Caesar what is Caesar's. Obviously you must recognize and understand that you live inside of a domain . . . therefore not to follow the laws and pay your taxes and give your tribute to Caesar . . . is wrong. If you were born into this

7. Boyd, *Myth of a Christian Nation*, 11.

> and this is what you are and you're a Christiaan, you should be a model citizen, or try to be. . . . But you have to remember, God is your king. You may have a president, but God is your king. . . . I think you should be a good citizen, but I think your duty also is to call out social injustice when you see it. When it's wrong it's wrong, and you should say it's wrong.

Emily's work and perspective necessarily involve a more universal set of political and social goals. It is not just the theological and moral aspects of nationalism that concern her. Working on climate change, a problem which recognizes no national borders, Emily faces the pragmatic frustrations brought about by nationalism. Solutions to the problem require international cooperation; as a Christian, Emily has to put Christian love of neighbor into concrete practice. "I feel very lucky to live in this country. I've been afforded a lot of freedoms. . . . But our problems are global," Emily explains. "And so if I'm a Christian who cares about environmental stewardship and protecting God's creation, and protecting vulnerable communities and the least of these from extreme weather impacts, I can't be nationalistic." The withdrawal of the United States from the Paris Climate Agreement by the Trump administration, under the auspices of an "America-first" perspective, "doesn't help my friend who lives in Fiji, whose island nation is already facing an existential crisis and will continue to see coastal villages destroyed unless we take greater action. And so the concept of nationalism can be very frustrating because if we really care to love our neighbor," we must remember that "our neighbor doesn't just live in the United States."

Although they've never met, Tessa would agree with Emily's perspective, as that mentality is what drives Tessa's refusal to take an "America-first" perspective despite her great love for her country. In her work employing refugee women, Tessa says, "The whole goal is to love people in my business. I hope what I am doing in my business is loving people and is indicative of the gospel."

Tammy, who runs Hope House, comes from a very patriotic military family and loves her country dearly. But she is very uneasy about nationalistic positioning: "I'll put my hand on my heart, and I love my country. I have a strong military background [and] my family is very patriotic. But I don't agree with nationalism, because I don't believe we are called to be Americans; we are called to be citizens of a greater kingdom. That means we identify with kingdom ethics that flip the idea of the American dream on its head." She gives the examples of refugees and immigration as an area where she sees her Republican and Democrat friends not really following those kingdom ethics and instead toeing the party line. "I don't really identify with either political party, because I don't agree with them . . . Neither one of them speaks to what I passionately care about—and I passionately care about removing the freaking oppression that is just rampant all over this land."

Recently, this issue of how we treat refugees has come into full focus in our culture, and it provides an excellent example of what allegiance to Christian values, over and above allegiance to the nation, might look like. In light of the Trump administration's attempts to significantly reduce the flow of asylum-seeking refugees[8] into the United States, some Christian groups have called for more sympathetic policies. We were moved to see evangelical Christian leaders exemplifying the kind of love that Jesus expresses in the gospels when they placed a full-page ad in the *Washington Post* in which one hundred evangelical leaders signed a letter addressed to President Trump and Vice President Pence expressing concern about the administration's refugee policies. The letter cited Jesus's treatment of hurting people and his clear teachings "that our 'neighbor' includes the stranger and anyone fleeing persecution

8. It's important to note here that we're talking about refugees, not immigrants in general. The word *refugee* in international law and understanding has a technical definition, as designated by the United Nations: "A refugee is someone who has been forced to flee his or her country because of persecution, war or violence. A refugee has a well-founded fear of persecution for reasons of race, religion, nationality, political opinion or membership in a particular social group. Most likely, they cannot return home or are afraid to do so. War and ethnic, tribal and religious violence are leading causes of refugees fleeing their countries" (UNHCR, "What Is a Refugee?"). The contention over legal and illegal immigration is strong enough; we assume that how we treat refugees should be an easier area of agreement for Christians.

and violence regardless of their faith or country." The letter sought an even broader inclusion in noting that "followers of Christ face horrific persecution and even genocide in certain parts of the world. While we are eager to welcome persecuted Christians, we also welcome vulnerable Muslims and people of other faiths or no faith at all."[9] This, we believe, typifies the kind of example Christians need to be for their country: a moral compass when the government's morality is questionable.

Identifying "Civil Religion"—and Attempting to Separate It from Christianity

The thing is: it's hard to be a moral compass when you have come to a place of conflating your religion with your political beliefs. If you can't separate one from another in the first place, it's difficult to determine how they might be dis-ordered, let alone how one should be critiquing the other morally. It seems to us that a chapter devoted to looking at the relationship between people's Christian identity and their national identity as Americans requires a discussion, even if brief, of what is called "civil religion." In an essay penned back in 1967, the sociologist Robert Bellah argued that there exists "an elaborate and well-institutionalized civil religion in America."[10] This "civil religion" (also called "civic piety" or "religious nationalism") is called such because it is constituted by functions and symbols in much the same way that certain functions and symbols operate in the world's religions, including Christianity. One author provides this set of examples:

> Civil religion involves beliefs (but no formal creed), events that seem to reveal God's purposes (most notably the American Revolution and the Civil War), prophets (especially Washington, Jefferson, and Lincoln), sacred places (shrines to Washington, Lincoln, and Franklin Roosevelt; Bunker Hill; and Gettysburg), sacred texts (the Declaration of Independence, the Constitution, and

9. Burke, "100 Evangelical Leaders."

10. Bellah, "Civil Religion in America," para. 1.

> Lincoln's Gettysburg Address), ceremonies (Memorial Day, Independence Day, Veterans' Day celebrations, and the pageantry of presidential inaugurals), hymns ("God Bless America" and "My Country, 'Tis of Thee"), and rituals (prayers at public events such as inaugurals and the beginnings of sessions of Congress and national days of prayer).[11]

It should be easy to see here that civil religion is distinct from Christianity precisely because it involves these national, not religious, functions and symbols. But the problem, in our view, is that civil religion is so ingrained in our American culture that we have become a people unable to see the difference between civil religion and the Christian religion—between devotion to flag and devotion to Jesus. We've conflated the symbols of civil religion with those of Christianity. This poses a big problem and an even bigger challenge. It's a problem because of the nationalism that undergirds civil religion, and as we've tried to argue above, in the nicest way we can, nationalism has no place in true Jesus-centered, Jesus-following Christianity. And it's a big challenge because it has been so ingrained in us that we don't even see it. It just doesn't register that there may be a conflict of interest between our devotion to our nation and our devotion to Christ. It's the air we breathe, so to speak. Saying the Pledge of Allegiance in our schools, celebrating patriotic holidays, wearing a flag pin on our lapel (or sporting flag-print swimsuits, for that matter)—these are all, in their own way, indicative of the forms of civil religion Bellah described fifty years ago. The South African Methodist pastor Peter Storey assesses the challenge that civil religion poses to American Christianity this way:

> American preachers have a task more difficult, perhaps, than those faced by us under South Africa's apartheid, or Christians under Communism. We had obvious evils to engage; you have to unwrap your culture from years of red, white and blue myth. You have to expose, and confront, the great disconnection between the kindness,

11. Smith, "Civil Religion in America," 3.

> compassion and caring of most American people, and the ruthless way American power is experienced, directly and indirectly, by the poor of the earth. You have to help good people see how they have let their institutions do their sinning for them. This is not easy among people who really believe that their country does nothing but good, but it is necessary, not only for their future, but for us all.[12]

We feel like we need to pause here and say afresh that we're *not condemning patriotic feelings* or the importance of shared national identity when it is working toward the common good, when it is inclusive and compassionate, when it doesn't limit our love for any of our neighbors across the street or across the world. We're not condemning America nor anyone's love for their country. We *are* condemning blind faith in it as some kind of savior or otherwise-perfect anything. Christians already have that, and it is not the nation-state. We recognize, as Donald Miller puts it, that "God is not in the business of brokering for power over a nation; [God] is in the business of loving the unloved and pulling sheep out of crags and bushes."[13] And because we recognize that, we also hope to convince our readers that any conflation, intended or unintended, of Christian values with state values and power is dangerous ground indeed for Christians:

> [Jesus] upset those in charge at the courthouse and the temple. He suggested they were not doing their jobs. He offered himself as a mirror they could see themselves in, and they were so appalled by what they saw that they smashed it. They smashed him, every way they could.
>
> One of the many things this story tells us is that Jesus was not brought down by atheism and anarchy. He was brought down by law and order allied with religion, which is always a deadly mix. Beware of those who claim to know the mind of God and who are prepared to use force, if necessary, to make others conform. Beware of

12. Quoted in Claiborne, Wilson-Hartgrove, and Okoro, *Common Prayer*, 361.

13. Miller, *Searching for God Knows What*, 194.

> those who cannot tell God's will from their own. Temple police are always a bad sign. When chaplains start wearing guns and hanging out at the sheriff's office, watch out. Someone is about to have no king but Caesar.[14]

American Values at Odds with Christian Values

It's important to be very clear here about some of the ways that American values and Christian values aren't compatible. That is not to say that American values are bad *per se*. They aren't. But they are not particularly *Christian* as we have attempted to define Christianity thus far in this book—as the authentic effort to follow Jesus's teachings. For example, the American narrative emphasizes individualism—and "rugged" individualism at that. Freedom and individual rights are connected to this idea: as an American, I am free to do as I please, for the most part, with little or no government restraint on me as an individual. America also values the pursuit of power through strength. A strong military and a strong economy are marks of our power and are the manner by which we protect our freedom—which is understood as freedom for Americans first (although all too often, we know that protection of freedoms and rights is denied to certain populations and groups within America).

Without arguing at all that freedom and rights and concern for the individual are negative values, we would argue that they are not to be understood as marks of the body of Christ. Jesus cared about individuals—very much so—but not as an end unto themselves. Rather, he cared for the individuals whom society had cast aside so that they could be restored to the community and society that had rejected them. And the notion of "freedom" as America understands it, we would argue, is a pretty incomplete understanding of freedom. Is a person who "chooses" to take a low-wage job in his community, where there are no other jobs to be had, really "free," even if we recognize that no one forced him to take the job? Is the choice between a low, non-living wage and

14. Taylor, "Perfect Mirror," 283.

starvation indicative of a person's "freedom"? On the opposite end of the economic spectrum, is the materialistic drive to have and consume, the insatiable compulsion to compete for the best car, the best house, the best gadgets, indicative of a person's freedom? Isn't that person enslaved to his desires, and therefore not "free"? As William Cavanaugh explains, "To speak of freedom in any realistic and full sense is necessarily to engage the question of the true ends of human life,"[15] which we spent several pages discussing in chapter 2. Timothy Keller contributes to this notion of genuine human flourishing, reminding Christians that some constraints on the pursuit of our individual wants and desires is actually a really good thing—which flies in the face of a more myopic notion of American "freedom." For Keller, being free of all constraints is unrealistic: "Whatever is the object of your meaning and satisfaction ultimately controls you. You are never your own master, never actually free in the contemporary definition. Something else is always mastering you."[16] The question, Keller explains, is not "Can I be free from constraints?" but rather, "What constraints will I accept?"

Finally, we should consider the American values of wealth and power and getting ahead through competition. Honestly, it feels weird to have to tell any reader who identifies as "Christian" that these things aren't exactly in line with Jesus's teachings. In his book *The Upside-Down Kingdom*, Don Kraybill explains how Jesus challenges these values in calling us to be vulnerable, to choose nonviolence, to love enemies, and to avoid seeking wealth for personal enrichment.[17] Where in Scripture do we see Jesus telling the disciples to try to earn the highest position or make the most money or compete with others to come out on top? Never—quite the opposite, in fact. Again, we're not criticizing hard work and recognition for hard work as necessarily *bad*—we, too, want to do our best, using our God-given talents and whatever gifts we may possess to pursue meaningful work and to provide well for our

15. Cavanaugh, *Being Consumed*, 25–26.

16. Keller, *Making Sense of God*, 110–11.

17. Kraybill, *Upside-Down Kingdom*.

families and communities—but we have to pursue these things in ways that don't conflict with authentic Christian values and teachings. We are citizens of America, yes—but we are citizens first of a different kingdom, with different values and goals. Boyd summarizes this well:

> To promote law, order, and justice is good, and we certainly should do all we can to support this. But to love enemies, forgive transgressors, bless persecutors, serve sinners, accept social rejects, abolish racist walls, share resources with the poor, bear the burden of neighbors, suffer with the oppressed—all the while making no claims to promote oneself—*this* is beautiful; *this* is Christlike. Only this, therefore, is distinct kingdom-of-God activity.[18]

When we begin to consider the differences in the value systems of both of these kingdoms, we may begin to see that it may not be possible to be a "good Christian" and a "good American" simultaneously.

So What?

So all of this is to say: if you feel compelled, go ahead and love the hell out of your country.[19] But don't allow love of your country to domesticate your faith. If you call yourself a Christian, it must be the other way around: Jesus must domesticate your views of the nation-state and call it to account when it is behaving badly. *It is possible to love your country but to choose consciously not to worship it!*

Our friend Paul, the Iraq War veteran, puts legs on this for us in a story about a fellow seminary student from another country. In conversation one day, this man told Paul, "I don't understand you Americans being proud to be an American. I'm not proud

18. Boyd, *Myth of a Christian Nation*, 103.

19. Okay, what we really mean by this is, like, love the *hell*—the violence, the uber-individualism, the rat race and the greed for more money, more power, more prestige, pursued at the expense of hurting others—right out of it.

of my country at all. We have one hero, and actually he wasn't a very good guy. I'm not proud of my country at all—but I love my country very much." Paul says that this conversation began to open up a new understanding for him about what it really means to love his country. He asserts that, as Christians, "we understand we're citizens of the kingdom and sojourners in this world." Christians believe that "government is ordained by God so that we have some order, but what we understand as Christians is that we cannot unconditionally support what our government does."[20] Paul argues that we must understand the weight of the responsibility Christians have in speaking out against the nation's actions when those actions are unjust, cruel, or otherwise wrong; and when we do speak against those injustices, "we have to understand, and our country has to understand, that we're not saying we hate our country, but that we love our country enough to be the conscience of our nation. And I think that this has to be the role of the church."

What Paul finds helpful—to bring things back full circle to the persecuted-church thing discussed earlier—is to be reminded of the martyrs of Christianity. Coming from an Orthodox perspective, Paul notes the many Orthodox and other martyrs who were executed or exiled for speaking truth to power. Paul believes we have lost the spirit of martyrdom:

20. A good and recent example of this is the defense by US Attorney General Jeff Sessions of the Trump administration's separation of migrant children from their parents at the US-Mexico border. On June 14, 2018, Sessions cited Romans 13, which argues for lawful obedience to the governing authorities, as the biblical basis and justification of the separation policy. In a nutshell, Sessions was arguing that if migrant parents don't want their children taken from them, they shouldn't try to enter the United States. Regardless of a Christian's views on immigration, and irrespective of whether a Christian leans left or right on political and social issues, lying to immigrant parents about what was happening to their children (as was reported by multiple news sources) and then taking children and detaining both parents and children in separate, undisclosed locations is, in our view, unjustifiable under any circumstances. That Sessions would use the Bible to justify the policy is beyond our comprehension, and we believe that Christian leaders and laity were absolutely correct in the loud and strong public outcry against the policy, which was eventually reversed.

> Christians in America are really laying down their faith instead of leading . . . Christians in America have lost their fervor and certainly their spirit of martyrdom that our early Christian brothers and sisters had. Instead of us being firm in our faith and saying, "this is wrong" and "that is acceptable," we are allowing secular forces to dictate to us how we should act, what we should do, what we should say, and what we should accept. I don't see us being the conscience of the state but rather the state dictating to us who we should be.

Paul believes that this is the reason so many Christians have left their faith and why so many non-Christians are disinterested: "People get a sense when dealing with lukewarm Christians that this isn't really of God. . . . We've watered ourselves down and we lose who we are, we lose grace, and we step outside God's world."

Compromising our faith, losing who we are, and being uncertain about what and who we are for—maybe that's the best definition of what it means to be a crappy Christian.

We want to conclude here with this thought: if our models of Christian faith have convinced us of anything in this chapter, it is that we need to stop seeing our faith through the lens of both our patriotism and our partisan political perspectives. We need to start seeing political issues, leaders, parties, and policies through the lens of Jesus's teachings. Period. That's way harder than it sounds, by the way. It means that when we talk about war, economics, gun control, abortion, poverty, healthcare, education, taxation, sex and sexuality, immigration—you name it—we have to reject the temptation to toe the party line and be willing to critique the system that has duped Christians into thinking that they can align their faith with the right or the left or the center without compromising that faith. That is to say: sorry, friends. Wherever you fall on the spectrum of far-right conservativism to far-left liberalism, you have had to compromise the teachings of Jesus. Perhaps if we could start by recognizing that—if we stopped being crappy Christians and worked harder to be a little more like the folks we've come to know through this book—we might find ourselves humbled enough to sit down with other Christians to work toward figuring out what a Jesus-centered perspective on these tough political and social issues might look like. We might figure out what we can be *for* rather than being against each other.

A Jesus-centered perspective of compassion, kindness, love, mercy, service to the marginalized, and humility are, we believe, aspects of a restorative and redemptive social order. We turn now to a discussion of how our models' active faith, compassionate love, and rightly ordered allegiances are contributing to the biblical concept of restoration and redemption.

5

Redemption and Restoration

The ministry of reconciliation includes evangelism, which breaks down barriers between God and humankind, and it also includes social action designed to break down the barriers of prejudice and injustice that drive people apart. It includes working for peace with people who are our obvious enemies, and it includes mending relationships on a daily basis with those we care about most. It involves learning how to love God better, and it involves loving the natural world too. All of this is included in the salvific work of reconciliation. Salvation is thus extended to all of life and is not limited to the spiritual dimension.

~ Douglas Jacobsen and Rodney J. Sawatsky, *Gracious Christianity: Living the Love We Profess*

By doing the work Jesus calls us to, we empower ourselves and others to see and imagine the potential for redemption in ourselves, in others, and in systems and structures. And when we can see or imagine that redemption it inspires us to do more or to view things in a more positive way.

~ Rick Polhamus

Introduction

It's easy to look at the current state of the world and feel a little hopeless and helpless. Christians on both sides of the political and social divide are torn, anxious, and angry. How are they supposed to talk about hope, restoration, and redemption when the levels of angst and division and general crappy-ness are *this* high?

And yet . . . that's what kingdom work is about, isn't it? That's the heart of the gospel message. When Christians pray, "Thy kingdom come, thy will be done on earth as it is in heaven," they are expressing a profound hope of restoration, wherein God establishes, finally, God's kingdom on earth. When Christians proclaim, "Christ has died; Christ is risen; Christ will come again!," they are recalling the hope that grounds every other aspect of the Christian life. In our darkest hours, hope of redemption and the restoration of those things that are *good*—love, peace, justice, joy, compassion, and kindness—signify what Christians in any place and at any time can be *for*. The reality of a future redemption of all the crappy-ness we see and experience is the driver of that Christian hope.

Emily clearly articulates this notion when she talks about the hope she maintains as she works on Capitol Hill to bring people together around the issue of climate change:

> I think of redemption as transforming something negative or challenging into something beautiful, just, and made new. And as a Christian, I believe that there is always hope and the possibility of transformation, even when it feels impossible. One of the reasons I find lobbying in a nonpartisan way to be so transformative is that the very act of engaging respectfully with those with whom I disagree demonstrates that redemption of our broken system is possible. Our climate and earth is being destroyed, yet I find hope and deeply believe in the capacity of our legislators to pass policies to heal and restore our world. By lobbying and building relationships with both Republicans and Democrats—even climate change deniers—I keep open the possibility that it's not

> too late for legislators to change course and work towards the solutions we so desperately need.

For Tammy, these kinds of ideas are built into the very name of the shelter she provides for abused and addicted women: Hope House. As she explains it,

> We believe that our efforts help to push back against the darkness by shining the light of hope. Hope is practical, it's tangible: in the shower they get to take, in the food they get to eat, in the washing machine they get to use, and in the fellowship we endeavor to draw them into. Hope is where the rubber meets the road. By offering our guests a place to rest from all the chaos caused by homelessness and uncertainty, we give them a chance to experience peace, order, and quietness, but also respect. . . . All these things contribute to restoration, first, of her precious dignity, then her time, then her opportunities and then hope for a better life.

This hope of redemption is critical to our models' approach to their work and the role they play as Christians living out their faith in the world. As such, it calls the rest of us to something similar in our own lives and circles of influence. Before we delve further into that, however, we need a fuller understanding of what we mean by "redemption." So let's begin where Christians should always begin for grounding their perspectives: with a biblical basis.

Biblical Redemption as Individual and Societal

Our goal here can't be an exhaustive treatment of biblical notions of salvation. Lots of other (and frankly, far smarter) folks before us have done that work. But we do want to highlight a few points that we think make the case for a "both-and" view of what it means to be "saved" or redeemed. If we think of redemption only in terms of personal salvation or only in terms of societal transformation, we miss the biblical boat. Christians are called to both. Individual salvation and the redemption of the entire world, including nature and societal structures, are inextricably linked in the restorative, reconciling work that we believe God intends for the world.

The gospel narratives are chock-full of examples of Jesus connecting with individual people and asking them to make a 180-degree shift in their thinking and behavior. We see this in the story of the Samaritan woman at the well (John 4:4–42), where an encounter with Jesus leads to the woman's transformation—a transformation so powerful that she goes off to tell her friends about it, and they in turn become followers.[1] The story of Zacchaeus (Luke 19:1–10) relates the radical transformation of one of those tax collectors we talked about in the previous chapter—the guys who were considered traitors because they were Jews working on behalf of the Roman government to collect taxes from their community, which were in turn used to rule over the Jews. Zacchaeus is so astonished by Jesus that he voluntarily gives half his riches to the poor and pays back four times the amount to anyone he cheated. "Today salvation has come to this house," proclaims Jesus as a result of Zacchaeus's conversion of both heart and behavior. The Apostle Paul himself undergoes this salvific transformation. We meet him in the New Testament as Saul, a Jewish leader who wreaks havoc on the early Christians, gleefully overseeing the death of the martyr Stephen (Acts 7:58—8:1), dragging Christians out of their homes and hauling them to prison (Acts 8:3), and generally "breathing threats and murder against the disciples of the Lord" (Acts 9:1). But his encounter with the risen Christ on the way to the town of Damascus leads to a total conversion in his worldview and in his actions, and he becomes the greatest proselytizer for Christianity in all of church history.

But these individual conversion stories are only one part of what "following Jesus" looked like in the first decades of Christianity. It seems important to note that "Christianity" wasn't called "Christianity" in the years following Jesus's work and ministry and eventual crucifixion. Following their experience and understanding of the resurrection, people referred to the faith as the "Way."

1. It may be worth noting that the Eastern Orthodox tradition recognizes the Samaritan woman as a saint of Christianity: Saint Photina.

A "way" implies a path that one takes or follows, or a journey or a route or even perhaps a set of directions to get from one point to another destination. If Christianity were solely about that moment of conversion, maybe the early church would have referred to themselves as the "Moment" or the "Turning Point" or something similarly static that signified the instant of conversion rather than all that comes after that conversion.

Don't get us wrong: the reality of personal transformation is critical in the Christian tradition. Many Christians can point to a significant moment or moments in their lives, sometimes as powerful as the biblical examples noted above, that they think of as transformative for their Christian walk or their understanding of what it means to become a disciple. But the problem we see with a whole lot of contemporary American Christianity is the overemphasis on that *moment*. Discipleship is a process, not a moment. Analogously, it's like focusing so much on the wedding day that a couple forgets about the hard work of marriage, and then they're surprised to find that the marriage doesn't stick. So, too, an overemphasis on the moment and not what comes after can be detrimental to the Christian life.

John Wesley, the founder of the Methodist tradition, recognized this in his teachings about soteriology (just a fancy word for the study of salvation). Wesley saw the moment of justification as undeniably important, yes, but his teachings about the process of sanctification—literally, "being made holy"—were central to all the rest of his work. His emphasis on pursuing holiness through discipleship was the basis of his work to build small communities of Christians in eighteenth-century England—communities in which people could support one another in the Christian life, hold one another accountable, serve the least of these, and disciple others into an authentic Christian life. The New Testament letter of James drives home the notion that what comes after our transformational moment is critical, as it in many ways provides the proof of the power and strength and authenticity of that moment:

> What good is it, my brothers and sisters, if you say you have faith but do not have works? Can faith save you? If a

> brother or sister is naked and lacks daily food, and one of you says to them, "Go in peace; keep warm and eat your fill," and yet you do not supply their bodily needs, what is the good of that? So faith by itself, if it has no works, is dead. But someone will say, "You have faith and I have works." Show me your faith without works, and I by my works will show you my faith. (Jas 2:14–18)

In our view, our work and participation in our own sanctification and our activity flowing from and reflective of our faith is kingdom work, and every person who claims to follow Christ is called to participation in that work. Kingdom work is about participating in the redemption not just of people but of the entire creation, with the end goal of a new heaven and earth. "For the first Christians, the ultimate salvation was all about God's new world, and the point of what Jesus and the apostles were doing when they were healing people . . . was that this was a proper anticipation of that ultimate salvation, that healing transformation of space, time, and matter."[2] This broader view of salvation clearly includes the redemption of the systems in which people live and function. This is what Paul is getting at when he writes in the letter to the Romans that "the creation waits with eager longing for the revealing of the children of God; for the creation was subjected to futility, not of its own will but by the will of the one who subjected it, in hope that the creation itself will be set free from its bondage to decay" (Rom 8:19–21). This, from our reading of the Bible, means that it's not just individual people who need redemption, but *everything*, including the systems and institutions that hurt those people in this life.

In their accounts of Jesus's work and ministry, the gospel writers seem pretty clear about this. Over and over again, we see Jesus critiquing the systems and structures that take advantage of people, that hurt them physically, and that are indicative of injustice by one group against other groups in first-century Jewish society. In John's gospel, a societal hierarchy that had developed laws allowing men to kill adulterous women seems to be turned

2. Wright, *Surprised by Hope*, 198–99.

on its head as Jesus tells a group of Pharisees that only those who have never committed a sin may participate in stoning a woman caught in adultery (John 8:3–11). Add to this the way Jesus talked with and treated women generally, and we're left with an image of a Messiah who worked to undo the hyper-patriarchy of his time. In constantly chastising the disciples for arguing about who's better (Luke 9:46) or should sit at his right hand (Mark 10:35–40), or how everything they've been taught about leadership is all wrong (Mark 10:42–45) and then washing their feet (John 13:1–17), Jesus appears intent on overturning hierarchies about power and prestige. And if Jesus cared only about converting individuals in order to save them and was unconcerned about systems of manipulation and oppression, why would he have bothered with that whole incident in the temple compound, where merchants were exchanging Roman money for Jewish money, selling animals for sacrifice, and generally taking advantage of people by putting a commercial spin on their desire to worship? What he sees leads him to a righteous anger out of which he causes quite the ruckus (Mark 11:15–17). Right after that, Jesus offers praise for a poor woman giving "out of her poverty" and condemns those who give "out of their abundance" (Mark 12:41–44). We also have the example of the earliest Christians, as reported in the first few chapters of Acts, whose experience of Jesus led them to community-wide sharing, hospitality, and economic equality wherein people were selling their possessions and sharing the proceeds with those in need (Acts 2:44–45), and there was thus "not a needy person among them" (Acts 4:34).

We could go on and on. But you get the picture. Authentic redemption, according to the Bible itself, is not just about "saving souls." Neither is it just about fixing societal structures and institutions. If we take the fullness of the gospel message seriously, which means the eventual establishment of a new heaven and a new earth, we recognize that it is always about both.

Delving Further into the Fullness of the Gospel: Or, What *Would* Jesus Do, Anyway?

It seems to us that the majority of mainstream Christianity in America sort of "gets" the personal salvation part. What concerns us, and what we in some sense really intend for this chapter to be about, is getting Christians also to grasp the second part: the redemption of the social realm, which includes political and economic systems, cultural norms and values, and all the other aspects of how societal life is organized. We see the models of Christian faith whom we've been highlighting in the previous chapters as living in their own way into that two-part understanding of full-gospel, wholly redemptive Christianity. We want to spend a few minutes here emphasizing the social-redemption part of the gospel message, since that's the part we see a lot of Christians missing. By grounding this emphasis in a quick historical framework of the "social" gospel in America, we hope to provide some context for our concerns and perhaps, along the way, help Christians living in the current moment understand that they too are called to work for redemption and restoration of the systems and institutions that constitute so much of daily life.

A Short History of the Social Gospel

Back in the 1990s, the "What Would Jesus Do?" movement began in a small town in Michigan, when a church youth leader began encouraging her youth group members to think about what their lives would look like if they paused to consider what Jesus would do in every instance, every action, every decision of their day. Nearly three decades later, you still see people wearing the WWJD bracelet, or sometimes a T-shirt or button or other accessory. It's a big enough cultural phenomenon that most Americans know what WWJD stands for even if they didn't grow up in a church, and people know that the person exhibiting the logo identifies as a Christian.

But what most people don't know is that the idea behind the WWJD phenomenon of the nineties was nothing new. The Michigan youth leader, Janie Tinklenberg, reports that she would occasionally pull a certain novel from her office bookshelf to read, and one day she had a revelation of sorts that the book's message would make for a great discipleship lesson with her youth. The book? *In His Steps*, written in 1896 (yeah, a whole century before Tinklenberg and her youth group started the WWJD thing) by Charles M. Sheldon. It's the story of a pastor who challenges his congregation to consider very seriously for one full year what Jesus would do as they went about their daily activities. That commitment shifts the church members' interpretation and implementation of Christian faith from a personal-salvation-only focus to a social emphasis, which in turn revolutionizes the town in addressing the social ills that plague it.

Sheldon was instrumental in what came to be called the Social Gospel movement at the turn of the twentieth century in America. But he was not the most significant promoter of the movement. That designation goes to Walter Rauschenbusch, a German-born Baptist pastor whose ministry in the Hell's Kitchen area of New York City in the early 1900s exposed him to such poverty and terrible conditions that he developed a "theology for the Social Gospel," encapsulated in his book by the same title.[3] This was before the organized labor movement, when there were still no laws limiting hours worked or protecting people in the workplace, and when even young children worked beside adults in factories in horrendous and unsafe conditions. Rauschenbusch's experience of serving an impoverished community whose misery was made worse by an exploitative labor system led him to theologize that the gospel *had* to be about more than the redemption of an individual's soul. A "pie-in-the-sky" notion that people should just suffer silently and submissively through their crappy earthly existence in order to reach heavenly salvation wasn't good enough, in Rauschenbusch's view. His reading of the Christian Scriptures, especially Jesus's teachings about the kingdom of God, led him to emphasize the

3. Rauschenbusch, *Theology for the Social Gospel*.

work to be done by Christians in the social realm to participate in ushering in that kingdom. Importantly, Rauschenbusch acknowledged and even insisted upon the importance of personal salvation: "It is always a great and wonderful thing when a young spirit enters into voluntary obedience to God and feels the higher freedom with which Christ makes us free. It is one of the miracles of life." However, argued Rauschenbusch, "a salvation confined to the soul and its personal interests is an imperfect and only partly effective salvation."[4] We need a fuller understanding of the gospel, argued Rauschenbusch:

> Complete salvation . . . would consist in an attitude of love in which [a person] would freely co-ordinate his [*sic*] life with the life of his fellows in obedience to the loving impulses of the spirit of God, thus taking his part in a divine organism of mutual service. When a man is in a state of sin, he may be willing to harm the life and lower the self-respect of a woman for the sake of his desires; he may be willing to take some of the mental and spiritual values out of the life of a thousand families, and lower the human level of a whole mill-town in order to increase his own dividends or maintain his autocratic sense of power. . . . [S]alvation must turn us from a life centred [*sic*] on ourselves toward a life going out toward God and [people]. God is the all-embracing source and exponent of the common life and good of [hu]mankind. When we submit to God, we submit to the supremacy of the common good. Salvation is the voluntary socializing of the soul.[5]

In Rauschenbusch's work, we can hear Matthew 25 and the letter of James and lots of other passages cited earlier, echoing down through two millennia, can't we?[6]

4. Rauschenbusch, *Theology for the Social Gospel*, 95.

5. Rauschenbusch, *Theology for the Social Gospel*, 98–99.

6. We also see it lived out by Martin Luther King Jr. and his colleagues in the civil rights movement; if you'd never heard of Walter Rauschenbusch before reading this chapter, you probably don't know that his work and his theology of the Social Gospel had a significant impact on King when King studied the Social Gospel while attending Crozer Theological Seminary from 1948 to

A Whole Gospel for a Divided World

So why, you might wonder, doesn't American Christianity look like this? Well, there are some important historical explanations having to do with politics and dominant social/ethical paradigms and Christian infighting (sound familiar?), and while we don't have the time and space to address that here, we certainly encourage you to read about this in any good text on American church history. In her fantastic book *The Very Good Gospel: How Everything Wrong Can Be Made Right*, Lisa Sharon Harper briefly documents some of the reasons for American Christianity's contemporary shortcomings. She provides the historical background in her assessment of what she terms "the divided gospel" that resulted in the early 1900s when the white American Protestant church split into conservative evangelicals, who focused on personal salvation, and the liberal church, which focused on social reform. "On both sides of the divide, the gospel was thinner than before, containing only a fraction of its power and of God's purposes for the world." A "thin" gospel, according to Harper, sees no need to be transformed by deep engagement with the Scriptures or the community of faith. A thin gospel is marked by a lack of "serious study and reflection" and instead "skims the surface of sacred texts, using what seems applicable in the moment without connecting the dots."[7] And a thin, divided gospel—and the community that is susceptible to manipulation by it—is incapable of speaking and living the prophetic nature of the gospel, with all its hope of redemption, reconciliation, and restoration, in the current moment.[8]

In his book *Whole and Reconciled: Gospel, Church, and Mission in a Fractured World*, Al Tizon adds to our discussion here about the need for Christians to reclaim a whole gospel by calling on Christians to pursue and live into both sides of the same

---

1951. The Social Gospel also has connections to the liberation theology movement of the second half of the twentieth century, wherein Latin American theologians and ministers interpreted the Second Vatican Council reforms in the light of the situation of impoverished Central American Christians.

7. Harper, *Very Good Gospel*, 10.

8. Harper, *Very Good Gospel*, 11.

gospel coin. Tizon writes of his two experiences of the gospel which "more than hint at the scope of God's transforming work; they demonstrate the gospel's transforming power in sinful human hearts and broken social systems that cause inequity, poverty, and injustice."[9] He recounts his conversion experience in his teenage years, which led him out of what he now considers a meaningless, substance-abusing, perfectionist life to an intentional pursuit of God. But Tizon also references his "born-again *again* experience,"[10] which led him to an understanding of the need for salvation and redemption of all things, not just his own soul.

Active Gospel Agents in a Broken World

Participating in God's Redemption of Souls and Systems

So authentic Christianity requires that we recognize our redemption as both personal *and* societal. It's about individual people *and* it's about the broader world in which individuals live and function. In *Gracious Christianity: Living the Love We Profess*, Jacobsen and Sawatsky put it succinctly: "At its core, personal salvation is the process through which we internalize God's love for us so that we, in turn, can externalize that love to others. When we enter the path of salvation, we are taken up into God's great work of love and re-creation, and we are given the opportunity to become active agents in that process of reclaiming and reforming the world."[11]

"Great," you say. "So what might that look like?" It's time now to return to the heart of this chapter: highlighting the ways our models of faith understand their own work and journeys as contributing to a bigger picture of redemption and restoration.

While Ron's work with recovering addicts is very much about personal transformation, it doesn't end there. Ron sees his work at Sugartree Ministries as participation in "kingdom work

9. Tizon, *Whole and Reconciled*, 58.

10. Tizon, *Whole and Reconciled*, 59.

11. Jacobsen and Sawatsky, *Gracious Christianity*, 64.

on many levels"; these include fulfilling Matthew 25, where the Bible identifies service to Christ directly with service to the poor and marginalized, and working in the recovery program, which emphasizes "restoring people from a seemingly hopeless situation." As Ron says, redemption in his context is understood as "more of a destination" that one pursues on one's journey. His work with Sugartree has created within him habits and practices of living out those values beyond that environment and community. "I try to practice this in all aspects of my life," he says, "and when falling short, [I have] to get up and try again."

In her work to bring people together on issues related to climate change, Emily feels she is engaging in redemptive, kingdom-pursuing work. In the midst of extreme political and social division, Emily works across those divides in transformative efforts to change how people see climate change and its ramifications. Her vision of restoration is one that involves strengthening democracy through communication between people and lawmakers:

> When I train individuals how to lobby their elected officials, I see that as redemption work. In my mind, a redeemed community is one where every person's potential is fulfilled, the environment is clean and resilient, and the community is at peace. But additionally, community members have the tools to articulate their needs to elected officials, and the elected officials who represent them actually listen to every person who shares their stories and concerns. These leaders then make structural changes that would better serve the needs of their community, and joyfully work to reflect those desires in changes to our laws. In a redeemed community, everyone gets a voice at the table, and is heard equally by their elected representatives. So by teaching other people how to effectively communicate their needs to people in power, I'm hoping to build a healthier democracy and help empower people to work themselves to create Christ's kingdom on earth.

Julio's work at the intersection of immigrants' rights and protections and racial justice has led him to understand redemption as "coming back to a certain level of wholeness or balance." He argues that, while the world "has produced social structures that are meant to be oppressive to many," the Bible teaches "that when Christ came, he wanted us not only to deal with the spiritual health of people, but also their physical and emotional wellbeing." Julio believes he is called "to help as many people of the world" as he can and "to help make our world a better place for all that are alive now and in the future." When we first introduced Julio in chapter 1, we reported that he sometimes feels out of place in his work for social justice, peace, and equality because his Christian community doesn't really support his efforts, and his secular associates don't really understand how his faith relates to the peace and justice work they do and are leading the way on together. But, says Julio, "My dream, and I believe God's dream, would be for Christians to lead the charge on true equity and peace. Realistically, I realize that not everyone will accept Christ, but I believe that all of us can restructure how we view the world"; then, we "do everything we can to uphold peace, equity, and justice" by "actively doing everything possible to help mend the situation."

Rick's story, too, points to the connections between personal and societal redemption and the deep connections that exist there. Rick understands his own redemption to be connected to his work to build peace between enemies one relationship at a time.

> I hope that the things I do in CPT and in my personal life make a contribution to the redemption of people. In CPT it is an essential element of the work we do on several levels. . . . On a personal level I think that the granting of salvation/redemption is strictly God's job. My role is to do the things Jesus calls us all to do: heal the sick, feed the hungry, give shelter and comfort to the poor, help the prisoner become free (whether a literal prisoner or figuratively in society), address injustices, love God, love others, and love even enemies. And while doing these things may set the stage for redemption of self, others, or society, it is through the grace of God that the salvation comes, like Paul writes about in Ephesians. Paul also writes that we are created for good works and in the book

> of James, it says faith without works is dead. By doing the work Jesus calls us to, we empower ourselves and others to see and imagine the potential for redemption in ourselves, in others, and in systems and structures. And when we can see or imagine that redemption it inspires us to do more or to view things in a more positive way.

One of our favorite stories that Rick tells is about the kind of transformative redemption that can happen when we start operating from a more Christ-centered paradigm. We mentioned this story in brief in chapter 1, but it seems relevant and appropriate here to tell the story more fully.

In 2005, while on assignment in Palestine, Rick and his Christian Peacemaker Teams colleagues were videotaping Israeli contractors bulldozing a Palestinian home. Toward the end of the demolition, and with no provocation, Rick was violently assaulted by an Israeli soldier named Avi who was known for his brutality against Palestinians and anyone working with them. Because the assault was caught on video by another CPT member, Rick and CPT pressed charges in Israeli courts. The case eventually went to Israeli military court, where Rick would have to testify.

On the day of the trial, Rick arrived at court and was told to wait on a long bench outside the courtroom. After a few minutes, Avi came out of the courtroom and sat down at the other end of the bench. As Rick sat in that uncomfortable situation, he thought about the number of times he had taught in his adult Sunday school class about forgiveness, especially Matthew 18 where Jesus teaches that when someone sins against you, you should go to the person and try to resolve the issue. So, as Rick explains, "I stood up and walked down to where he was sitting. He looked up at me with a surprised look on his face. I extended my hand and said, 'Avi, I want you to know that I forgive you for what you did to me. And I am sorry that we have to go through this but the violence you have been doing has to stop.'" Avi responded by slapping Rick's hand away. Rick returned to his end of the bench.

During the trial, Rick told his side of the story, which was corroborated by the video evidence. At one point, Avi told his shocked lawyer that he wanted to cross-examine Rick. Avi asked Rick, "Did you ever see me do anything nice to anyone?" Rick responded, "Well, I have seen you be nice to your friends." Avi insisted, "That's not what I mean. Have you ever seen me be nice to others, like Arabs?" Rick responded, "Well, sometimes when there were internationals present, especially international press, I wouldn't say you were nice but you weren't acting mean either."

Rick was asked to return to the bench outside the courtroom. From there, he could hear what sounded like a scuffle and some angry shouting, followed by Avi's exit from the courtroom in handcuffs and escorted by military police. As Avi was led past Rick, he said, "The next time I see you, I will kill you."

Nine months later, Rick was in a quiet wing of the Tel Aviv airport waiting for an international delegation to arrive when he noticed a man walking rapidly toward him. As the man approached, Rick recognized Avi and immediately recalled the last thing he had said to Rick in the Israeli courthouse. There were no security guards nearby. To Rick's total surprise—and utter relief—Avi smiled as he walked up to Rick and, hugging him, said, "Rick, it is so good to see you here."

He went on to explain to Rick that he had changed Avi's life. Rick recalls the story Avi told him: "When he first was held in the prison, he thought about all the horrible things he would do to me if he ever saw me again. But he kept thinking about and was troubled by that memory of me coming over to him and saying that I had forgiven him. He said that it bothered him because I had seemed to do it in a sincere way, like a friend would. He started to think about how none of his friends were coming to visit him in prison. His girlfriend wasn't going to visit because she had left him when he started beating her when they had a disagreement. His family wasn't going to visit as they had essentially disowned him after Avi beat up his brother over something to do with a car. They had made it clear they would not forgive him."

Avi explained to Rick that Rick was "different." Rick had forgiven him, even though his loved ones hadn't, and had told him that the violence had to stop. All of this made Avi look internally and realize that he had treated others terribly, including Palestinians, whom he had begun to view as less than human. Avi had made a conscious decision to make positive changes in his life. He had apologized to his family and ex-girlfriend. He thanked Rick again, shook his hand, and the two made plans to meet for coffee in the future. Rick explains, "I have seen Avi a few more times over the years and while we will probably never be best friends, we have come a long way in our relationship. And I think about how he wasn't the only one changed. My faith is stronger and it is easier for me to see the opportunity to live that faith in any conflict." For Rick, this story illustrates the work of redemption in profound ways:

> On one hand I can feel that I aided in the redemption of Avi, although in the end it was and is his choice of actions and God's action that determines whether there is redemption for him. But seeing the potential for redemption in what happened with Avi inspires me to continue doing those things that were my part and also causes me to try to see that potential in other situations. It provides the hope that makes me keep trying to see that potential.

The Centrality of Authentic Community

In chapter 2, we spent some time talking about the importance of authentic community for our capacity to embody authentic Christian faith. We promised to return to that idea in this chapter, as the idea of building community is so central to what it means to usher in the kingdom through reconciliation with those who have been ostracized from the community by the hatred, oppression, exploitation, and even violence of one group against another. One of the things we really want to impress upon our readers is that Christians are to be *for* building community across all sorts of lines: social, political, racial, economic, gender, and even religious borders and boundaries. These boundaries are constructed only by our collective will to form them, and the only thing that keeps them standing is our lack of will to knock them over in true, authentic compassion that transforms all in the spirit of the radical hospitality of Jesus.

Each of our models talks about the importance of community in understanding their work as participation in the redemption of both souls and systems. Ron explains that Sugartree's work enlists volunteers from more than thirty different churches as well as community groups. For Ron, this reality "introduces a bigger picture philosophy of kingdom over doctrine and denomination" and reminds the serving community "that we are children of God following the example of Christ, driven by the Holy Spirit": a community that is "not perfect in action" but is doing its best, together, to serve those whom society deems worthless. Tammy says that, at Hope House,

> redemption and restoration begin when we open the door and *invite them in*. The invitation says, "We want you here and we care about what's going on," which is so much more than "Yeah, we have beds." We embrace our guests, we invite them into our community, and offer grace and emotional support for whatever comes next. We believe that if we bring kingdom ethics of mercy, humility, justice, honesty, and love to bear upon our guest during their time with us, we give possibilities a chance to grow.

And for Rick and his work with Christian Peacemaker Teams,

> bringing people together across divisions and helping them see the humanity of the other/enemy/opponent sets the stage for those people and communities to be redeemed. Also, the telling of stories about these actions and their results helps to break the stereotypes and misunderstandings that people have about one another, and this can cause relationships to be repaired or created and thereby expand Christ's kingdom. [This is] the beloved community.

We begin to see from these exemplars of Christian faith and service that as Christians participate in God's restorative activity in this world, there simply isn't room for some paternalistic, "let's go help those poor people" attitude. Participation in God's restoration of souls and systems requires humility and a pretty radical sense of equality with those we seek to lift up. It requires that we begin to view life from the point of view of the marginalized and that we see the dignity, humanity, and the very face of Christ himself in their faces and in their struggle.

Wrapping It Up

As we bring this chapter to a close, we recognize that it can feel a little overwhelming to be asked to think about what our own participation in God's redeeming work can or should look like. At the risk of sounding like a broken record, we need to say here again: there's no cookie-cutter approach. Large-scale good comes from broken people making small but meaningful choices about how they will participate in the restorative work that God's already doing. The great thing is that we get to pray and consider and discern what our participation will look like as we move through our lives. Our models chose particular paths, and as their own journeys of faith continue, their participation in God's redemption of souls and systems will continue to take new form and direction. The same calling, but along different paths, is open to the rest of us. What a gift to know that our lives on this earth are intended to be about so much more than material accumulation or being against people or even just pursuing our own happiness. We just need to live into it.

Wouldn't you agree?

Conclusion

How Not to Be a Crappy Christian

So . . . Now What?

Now comes the part where we provide a nice, neat, formulaic list of things you can and should do to make your life look more like the models described in this book and which will help you avoid the crappy Christian trap.

Except . . . no, we don't have a tidy formula, mostly because we recognize that human life is not tidy at all. It's messy and dynamic and so is each of our attempts to align our lives better with Jesus's teachings and to live lives that reflect authentic, Christ-centered faith.

But then . . . we're both teachers, and so we think it would be totally irresponsible to leave things here and not offer at least a few humble suggestions about concrete things that may be necessary for pursuing authentic Christian faith. Believe us when we say we're not trying to be preachy here; after all, we have no room to preach, since we've already noted several times that we ourselves are crappy Christians (but working on it). We're taking cues from the seven people we've discussed in the previous pages (who, incidentally, would probably tell you that they, too, are crappy Christians, although we'd beg to differ). In these last few pages, we want to go back to what we said in the introduction of the book: there is plenty for Christians to be *for* rather than *against*. We can be *for* things like community, love, costly discipleship, continual transformation, and lots of other good gospel values. It's a matter of choosing daily to live into an increasingly authentic Christian walk.

Crappy Christians, Unite

One of the key lessons from our models is that true Christian community is necessary for any authentic life of faith. Community is at the heart of the work that all our models do, and we want to be really clear about the importance of working out the gospel in unity with others. Although at some points we've written about our models' work as individuals, there are no Lone Rangers here. Each of them works in and through a community of servers and served, alongside other individuals who together make up a collective: Ron has the Sugartree community, Rick works with Christian Peacemaker Teams, Paul lives among and partners with the neighbors he serves through FOCUS Pittsburgh, Emily is aligned with FCNL staff and has found a supportive church, and so on. And when it's hard to find community, as is somewhat the case for Julio, we can really experience the added difficulty and challenge of pursuing embodied, radical love and keeping our loyalties in order. It can be lonely work, and we need others with us as we pursue it.

In this age of individualism, we need to recall that Jesus worked closely with a small group of dedicated followers because faith and service is best done in community. Yet you may know that it can be hard to find a church or group of Christians who are aware of their own crappiness and are together working to become better exemplars of Christian faith. We need communities of like-minded people to help us love our neighbors better. And if our church or group doesn't seem to be the community of love it's supposed to be, it's up to us to start leading and working with others in the right direction.

The really, really hard thing, though, is realizing that the community of love doesn't mean that we agree with everyone. Christianity simply cannot be used to pit us against others, and using faith as a way to further divide is, in our view, downright blasphemous. One of the best signposts of the kingdom of God is people who don't agree with each other on important issues deciding to maintain love and friendship anyway. When Christians divide over politics or social issues, they're divulging a dis-ordered loyalty to secular ideals rather than the sanctity of Christian love. We know—this is *massively* difficult. But then Jesus never told his disciples that following him would be a cakewalk. We shouldn't expect it to be for us two thousand years later.

Crappy Christians Need Discipline for Discipleship

Within and as part of community, authentic, whole Christianity needs discipline in order to grow. By "discipline," of course, we mean practice, not punishment. The words *discipline* and *discipleship* come from the same Latin root meaning "pupil." If we think about the ongoing learning and transformation that happen for individuals as they go from kindergarten to senior year, or about apprenticeship in fields like medicine or vocational training, perhaps we can make some connections to the notion of ongoing discipline needed for true discipleship within Christian faith.

If we take the "conversion moment and done" approach to salvation, then there's little space for considerations of "practicing" Christianity. One can just have their emotionally charged conversion moment and wake up the next day being a crappy Christian. To pursue *real* holiness ("sanctification," as we explained John Wesley's approach to it in the last chapter) requires practice. The notion of practice within Christianity isn't terribly different from the notion of practice needed to become a good athlete or to master an instrument. We're not good at playing piano the first day we sit down at one, no matter how committed we feel or how in love we are with the sound of piano music. Why would we think that something as critically important as redemption and living the Christian life is any different?

Most Christians, even if they don't actually practice them regularly, are familiar with types of devotional exercises that turn us reflectively inward, such as meditative/contemplative silence, Scripture reading, various forms of prayer, and journaling and other spiritual writing. These are critically important practices for Christians, as they are instrumental in growing the devotional faith of individuals or groups. But if, as we argued in chapter 5, redemption is both personal and social, then what practices help turn us outward even as we work on that inward piece? By way of example, we love the work of Grace Ji-Sun Kim and Graham Hill in their book *Healing Our Broken Humanity: Practices for Revitalizing the Church and Renewing the World*, which explores nine practices that build Christian community even as they push the church outward, toward transformation in the world and compassion for the marginalized and outcast.

Calling All Crappy Christians

In chapter 2, we included a quotation by Mother Teresa in which she says that one can find Calcutta anywhere, if one only has two eyes to see the misery and poverty and need of one's neighbors. We also discussed in that chapter the need to determine our Christian calling in light of the needs of the unwanted and unloved. We really want to drive this point home. While the witnesses of the "greats" in history—Martin Luther King Jr., William Wilberforce, Dorothy Day, Mother Teresa, and so many other famous Christian exemplars of authentic faith—retain their place as people to be emulated, our own callings may not be quite on that level. In fact, perhaps an emphasis on living the gospel vision in the ordinary, everyday of our lives is what's missing most for Christians. Speaking of Mother Teresa, here's a fun fact for those who find her particularly inspiring: Mother Teresa took the name "Teresa" from St. Therese of Lisieux in the Catholic tradition. Therese lived and died in the late nineteenth century and is celebrated for her emphasis on serving God and others in what she called "little ways." In recognition of two things—God's merciful love and her own inability to be perfect—Therese "translated 'the little way' in terms of a commitment to the tasks and to the people we meet in our everyday lives." While to the modern reader her life may seem "routine and ordinary," it was

> steeped in a loving commitment that knew no breakdown. It is called a little way precisely by being simple, direct, yet calling for amazing fortitude and commitment. . . . Her "little way" seems to put holiness of life within the reach of ordinary people. . . . St. Therese knew the difference love makes by allowing love to be the statement she made each day of her life.[1]

Large-scale or small, we are all called to a kind of public witness and work on behalf of those whom society casts aside. And we don't have to look far to find a place to serve. More than likely we already live, study, and work close to people who are sick, lonely, addicted, depressed, or hungry. People in need live in large cities, small towns, and rural areas. It's likely that someone is already working on those needs and could use your physical and/or financial support. If one thing is clear from our models' stories, it's that they didn't go far outside of their own daily circles and activities to discover the need. Ron went to the local soup kitchen and turned his past addictions into an opportunity to help others suffering from similar problems. Tammy was simply driving down her town's main street when she responded to her calling. Tessa returned home based on a gut-level feeling that her pursuits in the fashion industry weren't in line with her values and life's purpose. In some sense, these are all reminiscent of the "little way," and yet there is no little significance in the work of living the gospel values of compassion, love, and service.

Final Thoughts

As we come to the final words of this book, we have to wonder: did we write this for others, or did we write it for ourselves? We're painfully aware of what crappy Christians we are when held up to the light of a fuller recognition of the gospel. But the friends we've

1. Russell, "Her Little Way."

talked about here inspire us toward something better. We hope they have inspired you as well.

If, like us, you feel frustrated by much of the Christianity you see around you, we invite you to a fuller and, we argue, more authentic vision of faith. It's not easy. It's a vision that asks you to embody and live into gospel values of love and service. It asks you to love the same kinds of people Jesus loved, and with deep compassion and care. It asks you to reject social and political polarities and focus on bridging divides between people who have forgotten how to live reconciled lives. And it asks you to participate in the redemptive work that God is already doing in the world.

It's not easy. But what a gift to be part of that work.

Bibliography

Bellah, Robert. "Civil Religion in America." http://www.robertbellah.com/articles_5.htm.

Bonhoeffer, Dietrich. *The Cost of Discipleship*. Translated by R. H. Fuller. New York: Simon & Schuster, 1959.

Boyd, Greg. *The Myth of a Christian Nation: How the Quest for Political Power Is Destroying the Church*. Grand Rapids: Zondervan, 2005.

Brueggemann, Walter. *A Way Other than Our Own: Devotions for Lent*. Louisville: Westminster John Knox, 2017.

Budde, Michael. *The Church as Counterculture*. Albany: State University of New York Press, 2000.

Buechner, Frederick. *Wishful Thinking: A Theological ABC*. New York: Harper & Row, 1973.

Burke, Daniel. "100 Evangelical Leaders Sign Ad Denouncing Trump's Refugee Ban." *CNN Politics*, February 8, 2017. https://www.cnn.com/2017/02/08/politics/evangelicals-ad-trump/index.html.

Cavanaugh, William T. *Being Consumed: Economics and Christian Desire*. Grand Rapids: Eerdmans, 2008.

Claiborne, Shane. *The Irresistible Revolution: Living as an Ordinary Radical*. Grand Rapids: Zondervan, 2006.

Claiborne, Shane, Jonathan Wilson-Hartgrove, and Enuma Okoro. *Common Prayer: A Liturgy for Ordinary Radicals*. Grand Rapids: Zondervan, 2010.

Clapp, Rodney. *A Peculiar People: The Church as Culture in a Post-Christian Society*. Downers Grove: InterVarsity, 1996.

Day, Dorothy. *The Long Loneliness: The Autobiography of Dorothy Day*. New York: Harper, 1952.

Drane, John. "The Beginning of the Story." In *Introducing the New Testament*, 9–45. Rev. and exp. ed. Minneapolis: Fortress, 2001.

Ericksen, Adam. "The Politics of Palm Sunday." *Sojourners*, April 10, 2014. https://sojo.net/articles/politics-palm-sunday.

Ferry, Luc. *A Brief History of Thought: A Philosophical Guide to Living*. New York: HarperPerennial, 2011.

Giles, Keith. "Introducing Christians to Jesus." *Patheos Progressive Christian*, July 6, 2018. http://www.patheos.com/blogs/keithgiles/2018/07/introducing-christians-to-jesus/#IIyblsAKLsEIZlog.03.

Harper, Lisa Sharon. *The Very Good Gospel: How Everything Wrong Can Be Made Right*. Colorado Springs: WaterBrook, 2016.

Hauerwas, Stanley, and William Willimon. *Resident Aliens: Life in the Christian Colony*. Nashville: Abingdon, 1989.

Huddy, Leonie, and Nadia Khatib. "American Patriotism, National Identity, and Political Involvement." *American Journal of Political Science* 51 (2007) 63–77.

Isay, Dave. *Callings: The Purpose and Passion of Work*. New York: Penguin, 2016.

Jacobsen, Douglas, and Rodney J. Sawatsky. *Gracious Christianity: Living the Love We Profess*. Grand Rapids: Baker Academic, 2006.

Keller, Timothy. *Making Sense of God: An Invitation to the Skeptical*. New York: Viking, 2016.

Kim, Grace Ji-Sun, and Graham Hill. *Healing Our Broken Humanity: Practices for Revitalizing the Church and Renewing the World*. Downers Grove: InterVarsity, 2018.

King, Martin Luther, Jr. *Strength to Love*. Philadelphia: Fortress, 1981.

Kinnaman, David, and Gabe Lyons. *UnChristian: What a New Generation Really Thinks about Christianity . . . and Why It Matters*. Grand Rapids: Baker, 2007.

Kolodiejchuk, Brian, ed. *Mother Teresa: Come Be My Light; The Private Writings of the Saint of Calcutta*. New York: Doubleday, 2007.

Kraybill, Donald. *The Upside-Down Kingdom*. Harrisonburg, VA: Herald, 2011.

"Mahatma Gandhi Says He Believes in Christ but Not Christianity." *The Harvard Crimson*, January 11, 1927. https://www.thecrimson.com/article/1927/1/11/mahatma-gandhi-says-he-believes-in.

Manning, Brennan. *The Ragamuffin Gospel*. Sisters, OR: Multnomah, 2000.

McCullough, Donald W. *The Trivialization of God: The Dangerous Illusion of a Manageable Deity*. Colorado Springs: NavPress, 1995.

Miller, Donald. *Searching for God Knows What*. Nashville: Nelson, 2010.

Olsen, Ted. "The Positive Prophet." *Christianity Today*, January 1, 2003.

Piper, John. *Don't Waste Your Life*. Wheaton: Crossway, 2003.

Rauschenbusch, Walter. *A Theology for the Social Gospel*. Louisville: Westminster John Knox, 1997.

Romero, Óscar. *The Violence of Love: The Pastoral Wisdom of Archbishop Oscar Romero*. Compiled and translated by James R. Brockman. San Francisco: Harper & Row, 1988.

Russell, John F. "Her Little Way." https://www.littleflower.org/therese/reflections/st-therese-and-her-little-way/.

Schwehn, David R., and Dorothy C. Bass, eds. *Leading Lives That Matter: What We Should Do and Who We Should Be*. Grand Rapids: Eerdmans, 2006.

Smith, Gary Scott. "Civil Religion in America." *Christianity History* 99 (2008).

Taylor, Barbara Brown. "The Perfect Mirror." *Christian Century* 115.9 (March 1998) 283.

Tizon, Al. *Whole and Reconciled: Gospel, Church, and Mission in a Fractured World.* Grand Rapids: Baker Academic, 2018.

UNHCR. "What Is a Refugee?" https://www.unrefugees.org/refugee-facts/what-is-a-refugee/.

Volf, Miroslav. *A Public Faith: How Followers of Christ Should Serve the Common Good.* Grand Rapids: Brazos, 2011.

Wright, N. T. *Surprised by Hope: Rethinking Heaven, the Resurrection, and the Mission of the Church.* New York: HarperOne, 2008.